# Solutions For Anti-Black Misandry, Flat Blackness, and Black Male Death

This book deconstructs stereotypes about Black men through the exploration of their vulnerability, drawing attention to their demographic-specific issues and needs that are so rarely articulated.

Since the Black Power era, many Black men have responded with a Black identity affirming sensibility that sought to advance the cause of Black people. However, Black males have a need for race and gender-specific vocabulary that explains their experience with specificity, including concepts such as Black Masculinism, anti-Black misandry, and Black Andromortality, which seek to explain the experiences of Black males from the context of their lived experiences. Drawing upon empirical data, this volume offers policy solutions that challenge the institutional prejudices against Black males and the disproportionately high rates of death they face. Solutions are proposed to the outlined challenges, and chapters span topics such as social and family-based solutions, health, small-business support, law, and policy.

This book will be essential reading for researchers, professionals, and anyone interested in masculinity, gender studies, and Black Male Studies.

**T. Hasan Johnson** is an associate professor of Africana Studies at California State University, Fresno. He is also a founder and lead scholar at The Institute for Black Male Studies, located online at: www.instituteforblackmalestudies.com, and founder of the ONYX TV Network at: https://onyxchannel.network/. He is the developer of the concept of Black Masculinism and frequently publishes on anti-Black misandry, anti-Black male heterophobia, intra-racial misandry, and white supremacy.

**Leading Conversations on Black Sexualities and Identities**
Series editors James C. Wadley

*Leading Conversations on Black Sexualities and Identities* aims to stimulate sensitive conversations and teachings surrounding Black sexuality. Written by academics and practitioners who have dedicated their work to the distinctive sexual and relational experiences of persons of African descent, the series aims to provoke an enhanced understanding throughout the field of sexology and identify educational and clinical strategies for change. Amplifying issues and voices often minimalized and marginalized, this series is a continuation and expansion of inquiry and advocacy upon the complexities and nuances of relational negotiation, identity affirmation, critical discourse, and liberated sexual expression.

## Titles in the series:

**Sexual Health and Black College Students**
Exploring the Sexual Milieu of HBCUs
*Naomi M. Hall*

**Black Women, Intersectionality, and Workplace Bullying**
Intersecting Distress
*Leah P. Hollis*

**The Colonization of Black Sexualities**
A Clinical Guide to Relearning and Healing
*Anne Mauro*

**Sex Positivity and white-Sex Supremacy**
Ending Complicity in Black Body Erasure
*Carole Clements*

**Solutions For Anti-Black Misandry, Flat Blackness, and Black Male Death**
The Black Masculinist Turn
*T. Hasan Johnson*

# Solutions For Anti-Black Misandry, Flat Blackness, and Black Male Death

## The Black Masculinist Turn

**T. Hasan Johnson**

Routledge
Taylor & Francis Group
NEW YORK AND LONDON

First published 2024
by Routledge
605 Third Avenue, New York, NY 10158

and by Routledge
4 Park Square, Milton Park, Abingdon, Oxon, OX14 4RN

*Routledge is an imprint of the Taylor & Francis Group, an informa business*



ISBN: 978-1-032-52959-2 (hbk)
ISBN: 978-1-032-52963-9 (pbk)
ISBN: 978-1-003-40944-1 (ebk)

DOI: 10.4324/9781003409441

Typeset in Times New Roman
by Apex CoVantage Ltd

# Contents

# Foreword

As a Black father with two sons (ages 9 and 23), uncle to three nephews, and supervisor/mentee to few dozen Black male professionals, nurturing Black boys and men can be tough. What may make it difficult is that it is becoming increasingly harder to help my family navigate racism, systemic oppression, sexism, entitlement, colorism, and Blackness. What's compelling about Dr. Johnson's *Solutions For Anti-Black Misandry, Flat Blackness, and Black Male Death: The Black Masculinist Turn* is that he provides a prescription for all of us to rethink and reimagine gender expression so that we no longer have to subscribe to boxes that have held us hostage for centuries. He offers intriguing testimonies about how we can love ourselves, our children, and each other differently than what we have in the past. I think the challenge for us might be figuring out what brotherly love is, what it feels like, and whether or not we will run from it when we encounter vulnerability.

Dr. Johnson's book affirms our past, acknowledges our present, and creates emotive and relational pathways for us to be empowered. For this reason, this book is an essential read for us and the professionals who engage Black men through research, clinical care, or advocacy.

—*James C. Wadley, PhD*

# Part I

# The Scope of Black Male Life

# 1 Introduction

## The Black Gynocracy and the Black Gender Cold War

### I. Introduction

I have a son. He is currently graduating high school and is on the verge of leaving home. As a single father, this time period has been both much desired and yet much feared at the same time. And I am not alone in this, as a recent survey of a representative sample of around 3,000 adults explains:

> Americans are in general more worried about the prospects for boys than for girls, and for their own sons more than their own daughters, according to new data from the American Family Survey. Conservatives and men are most concerned about boys in general—but liberals are most worried about their own sons [and more so girls in general]. These views may be influencing political trends, and in particular the growing partisanship gap between men and women.
>
> (Reeves & Smith, 2022)

For my son and I, this moment is the culmination of years of preparation and training, but it still fills me with great concern regarding what he will confront and what may happen to him out in the world beyond my immediate sphere of protection. Because my son is a 6'10" Black male, the world sees him more for the threat they think he is than for the kind-hearted young man he truly is. But why mention this?

I share this with you to best frame my motivations for writing this book. The bulk of my work over this last decade has been about two things: one, to perform an accounting of the state of Black male life, and two, to explore what can be done to call attention to it while attempting to improve it qualitatively. This has been first and foremost applied to my son and the attempt to ensure his future but has spread to Black males writ large. This becomes extremely apparent when you casually peruse Black males' quality of life in America. Yet in far too many spaces, Black males' issues are ignored outright or significantly watered down.

DOI: 10.4324/9781003409441-2

But more than Black men's quality of life being largely ignored, there is the matter of Black men themselves coming to grips with how they are treated, seen, described, and thought of in society, in the Black community, and, at times, within the Black family itself. Here I refer to two concepts coming together to impact such males negatively: the gendered, low-boiling contempt Black men and boys face in families and the community (even from one another), and the institutional contempt they face in society via James Sidanius' *subordinate male target hypothesis*. The contempt, which will be dealt with in more depth later, often comes from within households and is often spewed from the mouths of parents and spouses, and in a gynopotestal family structure from female family members.

Sociologist Robert Staples helps explain the foundation for the idea of the gynopotestal family structure idea when he observes:

> A case which appears to fit a definition of the matricentric family is cited by Yehudi Cohen (1956). He studied a small community in Jamaica and actually found three family types. Of interest to us, however, is his description of what he calls the matripotestal family. This group is tri-generational and consists of a grandparent, an unmarried woman and her illegitimate children. The father is completely absent from this household.
>
> (Staples, 1972)

Thus, the matripotestal family structure consists of multiple generations of females who head their respective families under one primary matriarch, live under the same roof, and pass on family leadership generationally from mother to daughter. *Gynopotestal*, then, would refer to collectives of women who live under the same roof or in close-knit social settings where multiple families primarily depend on Black women who may or may not have blood ties. Hence, even in families where some aspect of a male presence is retained, this generally does not suggest a break from matriarchal status. Yet when males such as sons and other younger male family members are present, they may find themselves used as a resource for other households in the network of women. Repair work, manual labor, hauling, physical protection (the overall negotiation of violence), and even sexual services might be expected social practices. Regardless, each affirms Black males' status in families as servile to one degree or another.

The contempt mentioned earlier is passed down generationally as a response to generations of gynofocal policy that largely dismisses the need for Black boys and men and hyper-focuses on women and girls. Such can navigate society differently from their male counterparts in that they are more sought after for institutional and philanthropic support—made even more evident during the pandemic (e.g. Goldman Sachs, Mastercard, VISA, Google, and other such corporations [not including city, state, and federal policies] targeted women for job training, counter-homelessness efforts, and financial support).

Whether poor or middle-class, such women can access public welfare or college to a greater degree than their male counterparts. Many are spared from the fate of Black males, starting in K-12 practices that hyper-target Black boys for special education, detention, and even expulsion. While such Black girls clearly are more punitively mistreated than white girls to be sure, most (except for Native American boys) cannot claim to be hyper-targeted to the same degree as Black boys, despite the current trend to see heterosexual males as both toxic and thus morally less relevant to claims of extreme societal victimization. Such young males do not advance academically competitively and thus graduate high school to a lesser degree when you control for GED graduates. They attend higher education less and are hampered in the job market differently than others . . . and this process begins as early as preschool.

James Sidanius' notion of the *subordinate male target hypothesis* argues that such males are targeted because they are Black and male, thus subverting Kimberly Crenshaw's often lauded notion of *intersectionality*, which supports the notion that it is Black women who suffer most under the West's treatment of race, class, sex, gender, and more. Sidanius' argument puts intersectionality's validity to the test empirically, thus arguing that it is measurably such that Black males can be said to be the target of the worst treatment in society on many of the measures we perceive as important regarding the viability of any group. Carceral treatment, criminal and civil sentencing, leading causes of death, health, employment, income, wealth status, education, violence, intimate partner violence/homicide, rape, housing and homelessness, access to varied types of labor, political efficacy, wealth, family court impact (divorce and child custody most especially), fatherhood, forms of protest, marriage, and the history of institutionally based treatment are just a few areas we can assess.

But why compare Black girls and women to Black boys and men? Is this not counterproductive at best and mistargeting the true plight when critiquing Black females at worst? Is this not merely a cowardly gesture, attacking females and mischaracterizing the true victims in the Black community while avoiding the enduring legacy of white supremacy? Or is it simply a divisive measure extended out of a misguided attempt to blame Black women for the state of the community and avoid Black male accountability? Or worse yet, is it just a product of misguided rage at the author's (and others in agreement's) past relationships with women (i.e. "Who hurt you?")? Such questions have been raised before, so this text's conclusions have not been reached arbitrarily or without such opposition having been articulated. Know that this author does not attempt to do any of this. The types of intraracial comparisons used in this text elucidate how certain issues affect us to differing degrees, thus revealing that many are not just "Black" issues. Many are more nuanced in that they overwhelmingly affect one group much more than the other and thus require a slightly more specific lens to address the particularities of Black male life.

But these comparative reflections are performed for another reason in this study. They also explain a major reason Black men are starting to see their treatment inside and outside the Black community. It is not just structural and systemic as far as the larger society is concerned, but also learned and inherited within the community. There is a palpable disdain for Black men to which men are starting to respond from both the fringes of Black feminism to the everyday realities within coupling and family formation dynamics that have been intensifying for decades. Detected in experiences that range from ignored intimate partner violence/sexual assault practices in both boys and men to social expectations of men in dating, Black men find that they are hated . . . and often observe that they have been hated for generations—even within their own families. Their fathers and grandfathers too have been hated. The proverbial "you" as a Black man has been contending with hatred and social disdain intra-communally for generations, and it finally becomes most apparent when the most visible social protest organization in the last few decades profits from Black men's deaths while celebrating the idea of their very absence from Black families. The recognition of this disdain is the framework of this book. It is the foundation of the *Black Masculinist Turn.*

## II. The Black Gynocracy and the Weaponization of the Black Family Against Black Men

The advancement of Black women over their men is strategic and not accidental. As the economist Amadu Jacky Kaba observes,

> Unlike their female counterparts, who have seen tremendous economic, political, and educational gains over the past few decades. Black men have not seen great strides in their mobility from poverty or comparable gains in education.
>
> (Curry, 2017)

And:

> A priest some years back said, "If you want to destroy a community, or for that matter, a country, sow the seeds of distrust. It will not need an outside enemy. It will be destroyed from within."
>
> (Leader, 2017b)

What has taken place with white society and Black women is as diabolically brilliant a strategic move as the use of the Trojan Horse by the Greeks in war. It is also the foundation for a Black gynocracy in the United States. Kevin Cosby, president of historically Black Simmons College, designates five contexts that constitute the primary (all-Black) institutions of the Black community: schools, media, business, family, and the church. Ironically, Black males hold marginal positions in each category. Many are either failing out of K-12, being railroaded into special education, or being positioned into sports, while more Black women attend college and graduate school than Black males. To date, there is

> a 9 percentage-point gap between Black and Hispanic girls and Black boys compared to 4-point gender gap for white students and a 3-point gap for Asian students.
>
> In some states the on-time high school graduation rates for specific sub-groups are quite low. In Michigan, for example, only 61% of Black boys graduate high school on time, compared to 75% of Black girls, 81% of white boys, and 87% of white girls.
>
> (Reeves & Kalkat, 2023)

In terms of teaching, the gender divide is palpable. As of the 2015–2016 academic year, 80.1% of American public school teachers are white (Number and percentage distribution of teachers in public and private elementary and secondary schools, by selected teacher characteristics, 2017; Hansen & Quintero, 2022), with over 76% being women (USAFacts, 2020).

Black-owned media (not counting social media content) has largely been bought and sold after being inaugurated in the 1970s after years of racist exclusion since the 1930s. Sadly, by the mid-1990s, the gains from the new FCC policies that secured African Americans' access to media ownership had been reversed. By 2014, only two television companies were Black-owned. It can even be argued that the media has centered women as its primary audience for programming, as both Black Entertainment Television (BET) and TV One launched channels specifically for Black women (David, 2018).

The Black Church has witnessed a marked diminishment of Black male presence in the last 50 years, as much of the male congregation has either stopped going or has converted to Islam. Black men still serve as clergy, but the population of churches has always been mostly women. In business and entrepreneurship, Black men technically own more businesses (USAFacts, 2021). Still, Black women's businesses are growing faster with plenty of governmental, educational, and philanthropic support men's businesses do not get. Due to reproduction pharmaceutical technology, family court practices, and rates of single-parent communities, Black men do not control the Black family any more than they control any other institution in the Black community.

Much of the exclusion of Black men from these communal institutions is brought about by alien influences, as policy and institutional resources have made it so over generations. It is not an organic outcome due to the Black community's machinations. As a response, or lack thereof, there has not been a significant shift in Black social culture that has successfully prioritized Black male well-being in a manner that produced measurable gains on their behalf. The last period we saw such opportunity would be the Civil Rights era—particularly the Affirmative Action era. Unfortunately, at that point, white women rebranded themselves as minorities and took the lion's share of resources earmarked for Black America. Still, they made gains for women, evidenced by Black women who started to see marked advancements in education and white-collar employment. But did this advancement impact Black men? No. Instead, it created a new split in certain professional settings. Black women were said to have achieved "double minority" status—a status where they were said to be a benefit to employers seeking federal funds because they were both women and Black.

Such an advantage changes the reality of a relatively small community with little wealth. More to the point, divide-and-conquer strategies have impacted the Black community for generations. Whether it be elder generations versus younger generations, straight versus LGBTQ+, dark-skinned versus light-skinned, lettered versus the unlettered, poor/working class versus the upper-middle-class/elite, Black people descended from enslaved ancestors in the United States versus Black immigrants, healthy versus disabled, housed versus unhoused, or fit versus obese, each has contributed to the degradation of a racially coherent Black identity. And each is tied to structural economics, institutions, and policies that further entrench differences between intra-racial demographics. Yet despite each identitarian difference, few have as much impact as the tensions in gender dynamics amongst Black men and women.

Black women's relationship with white women (and white feminism) is key to their separation from Black men. The resources white women sought in response to their tensions with the white patriarchal dynamic in the white community were nominally offered to Black women. Particularly noticeable after the rise of feminism in the late 1960s, middle-class white women's entrance into white-collar labor and education offered to take Black women along with them in exchange for political advocacy. Riding off the heels of the Civil Rights Movement, this offered white women a moral rightness, a sort of currency that seemingly placed them on the right side of history. In exchange, poor Black women could access welfare resources originally earmarked for war widows since the 1940s. In contrast, middle-class Black women could better access higher education and low-level white-collar jobs (Nadasen, 2007).

## III. Matriarchy or Gynocracy?

During the Great Migration, when African Americans began migrating out of the South to the North, policies such as the *man-in-the-house rules* required that Black families in need of welfare entitlements could not have an able-bodied man in the home—whether it was the biological father or any other adult man (Kurwa, 2020). Such a policy had a debilitating effect on the Black family and serves as a perfect example of the *promotion/demotion thesis*, as the rules gave women an advantage that men did not receive, serving to bolster both an entitlement about what Black people could accomplish and a sense of Black female superiority. The *promotion/demotion thesis* is essentially the cause of the Black gynocracy. It explains why white society nominally advanced one gender while regressing the other by institutional means (early education coupled with early hyper-carcerality), crippling a community.

A matriarchy differs from a gynocracy in a very simple way. The former centers mothers as the central agents of the culture while the latter centers females across familial roles. Despite its importance, a gynocracy is not bound to motherhood as its defining factor. Girls and women become central at different levels and times. Still, historically, women-led families using either term are important to prove that such an entity exists. But I am not the first to address this. Reverend Dr. Martin Luther King, Jr. referred to this when he observed,

> Because the institution of marriage had been illegal under slavery, and because of indiscriminate sex relations, often with their white masters, mothers could identify their children but frequently not their children's fathers. Moreover, the women, being more generally in the house and charged with the care of the white master's children, were more often exposed to some education and a sense—though minimal—of personal worth. Hence a *matriarchy* had early developed. After slavery it persisted because in the cities there was more employment for women than for men. Though both were unskilled, the women could be used in domestic service at low wages. The woman became the support of the household, and the matriarchy was reinforced. The Negro male existed in a larger society dominated by men, but he was subordinated to women in his own society. The quest of the Negro male for employment was always frustrating. If he lacked skill, he was only occasionally wanted because such employment as he could find had little regularity and even less remuneration. If he had a skill, he also had his black skin, and discrimination locked doors against him. In the competition for scarce jobs he was a loser because he was born that way. His rage and torment were frequently turned inward, because if they gained outward expression their consequences could be fatal. The Negro father became resigned to hopelessness, and he communicated this to his children. Some men, unable to contain the emotional storms, struck out at those who would be least likely to destroy them. They beat their wives and their children in order to protest a social injustice, and the tragedy was that none of them understood why thc violence exploded.
>
> (King, 1967)

This text argues that the Black gender cold war is an extension of the "matriarchy" King refers to as having been developed in slavery. Black women's shift in worldview after the influence of feminism in the late 1960s, and the break-up of the Black family, are mostly a product of policy. But as policy has socialized Black women to assume leadership in families and communities (and somewhat ignore how their status came to be), it has simultaneously socialized Black men to serve as subordinates. Through poverty, drugs, limited opportunity, and more, Black males have already been socialized by lack to play few roles in society outside of those prescribed for them such as athletes, entertainers, criminals, or prison laborers. That some have found uncelebrated success outside of these societal tropes is remarkable and goes against our "programming."

## IV. The Impact of Misandric Policy

Like several key policies, the *man-in-the-house rules* played a significant role in breaking down the Black family, leading especially to the single-parent epidemic of female-headed households common in Black America starting in the 1970s. But this policy is not isolated. To reflect how policy has radically shifted the way Black women and men experience daily life in America, the following policies further split the Black gender experience. Poor Black women could more readily get access to Section 8; cash aid; tax credits; Supplemental Security Income (SSI); child support; transportation allotments; clothing allowances; diaper allowance; free childcare; free medical insurance; free gender-based mental health support; Supplemental Nutrition Assistance Program (SNAP) food stamps; The Special Supplemental Food Program for Women, Infants, and Children (WIC); Child Nutrition Program; subsidized housing; housing vouchers; public housing programs; medical insurance such as the Child Health Insurance Program (CHIP); Temporary Assistance for Needy Families (TANF); no-cost internet through the Affordable Connectivity Program (ACP); the Earned Income Tax Credit (EITC); the lifeline program run by the Federal Communications Commission (FCC) for discounted landline and cell phone service; Federal Public Housing Assistance (FPHA); and the Low-Income Home Energy Program (LIHEAP) to defer utility bills (HealthSherpa, 2022).

Furthermore, middle-class Black women have had greater access to kindergarten through high school college-track curriculums (they avoid special education), free college tuition, financial aid (Pell grants), college grants, childcare, investment from private companies in white-collar trade employment (e.g. Goldman Sach's $10 billion investment in Black women's future employment—see One Million Black Women, 2020), greater white-collar job access than Black men (64% to 41% respectfully), increased child support (percentage of greater income versus state distribution amounts), greater graduate school access, corporate internship programs, ability to run for office (due to increased education), and small entrepreneurial support earmarked for Black women (especially during the pandemic). White and Black women benefit from reduced criminal sentencing by 63% compared to men who commit the same crimes (Starr, 2015). Note that the 63% was in relation to men in general, so Black male criminal sentencing rates are worse for Black men (Demographic Differences in Sentencing, 2012; Ingraham, 2017).

Black women may not benefit from the following programs to the extent white women do, but they still have access to offices that have no male counterpart accessible to Black men. Offices and programs such as the Office of Women's Health in the U.S. Food and Drug Administration; the Office of Research on Women's Health in the National Institutes of Health (NIH); the Office on Women's Health in the Office of Public Health and Science; the Office on Violence Against Women; the Trafficking in Persons and Worker Exploitation Task Force; the Female Offender Branch, Criminal Section (Civil Rights Division), in the Federal Bureau of Prisons Correctional Program Division; the Office for Victims of Crime, U.S. Small Business Administration (SBA), in the U.S. Department of State Bureau of International Organization Affairs; the Center for Women Veterans in the U.S. Department of Veterans Affairs; and The White House Council on Women and Girls.

Such are the many ways institutions impact poor and middle-class Black families. Consequently, poor Black men often cannot leverage such resources to the same degree Black women can. That said, when you add law enforcement's capacity to side with women where the question of intimate partner violence is concerned, this provides women with another resource men do not get—a resource they can leverage out of revenge, anger, or coercion with few checks and balances. For example, when it comes to the frequency of female-initiated sexual violence, it generally goes far underrepresented. Lara Stemple et al. (2016) observe that concerning female perpetration and underreporting,

> There are numerous disclosure obstacles for victims of female perpetrators that ought to be kept in mind, particularly as reported in crime and other official reports (Denov, 2003b). Moreover, these disclosure obstacles . . . can operate to obstruct the ability of victims to access healthcare, recovery support, and legal redress (Davies & Rogers, 2006).
>
> First, the widespread perception of women as non-threatening complicates the way abuse is confronted by victims who experienced harm (Sandler & Freeman, 2009). Tellingly, researchers have found that victims who experience childhood sexual abuse at the hands of both women and men are more reluctant to disclose the victimization perpetrated by women (Sgroi & Sargent, 1993). Indeed the discomfort of reporting child sexual victimization by a female perpetrator can be so acute that a victim may instead inaccurately report that his or her abuser was male (Longdon, 1993).
>
> Male victims may experience pressure to interpret sexual victimization by women in a way more consistent with masculinity ideals, such as the idea that men should relish any available opportunity for sex (Davies & Rogers, 2006). Or sexual victimization might be reframed by observers

> as a form of sexual initiation or a rite of passage, to make it seem benign. In some cases, male victims are portrayed as responsible for the abuse. Particularly as male victims move from childhood to adolescence, they are ascribed more blame for encounters with adult women (Rogers & Davies, 2007).
>
> Some scholars have speculated that a reluctance to accept female perpetration may stem from the fact that this would destabilize understandings of safety. Because women have already accepted the idea that men pose a sexual threat, the notion that females may also be threatening is particularly unsettling. For lesbian women, the acknowledgement of sexual victimization within relationships "cracks apart the belief in a lesbian utopia" (Girshick, 2002a). Victimization by women in contexts of incarceration is also underreported. Even when abuse by female staff is reported through the proper channels, women accused of sexual victimization are more frequently allowed to resign than they are prosecuted for a crime, which parallels the more lenient treatment that female perpetrators in the broader community receive (Smith, 2012). The abuse of women inmates by other women is also often dismissed, described as merely a "cat fight," or explained away as an attempt by women to replicate outside family dynamics inside of prison (Stannow & Kaiser, 2013).

These benefits, whether based on policy or culture, provide women with immeasurable benefits that problematize Black men's lives. And each resource serves as an incredibly powerful lobby to not only promote entitlement in western (Black) women, which arguably exacerbates her expectations of men to compete with her "network" of resources to prove his "value" (and this doesn't include her family and friends, who also benefit in similar such fashion from the same resources). This process alone may have impacted declining marriage rates, as it likely disincentivized many Black men to marry.

This bifurcated treatment of Black men and women regarding policy access has also made dating, mating, marriage, and family formation more difficult over the generations. For example, to match value, a man living the same quality of life as a woman who earns much less (or may not even have employment) may have to earn tens of thousands more to compensate. This is made more difficult in that some women ridicule Black men who have not achieved as much largely due to not receiving the same types of policy benefits. In contrast, others overlook men who may earn more through blue-collar labor (and have no debt due to education) but lack the status of advanced college degrees. Thus, most Black men are often expected to meet unrealistic standards to be considered worthy of dating and have to be in the top 10% of all earners making over $100,000 per year to be considered viable candidates. Considering the state of Black wealth and the absence of inherited Black capital, this is a monumental task for the average Black male. Such leaves individual men to compete with the government for too many a woman's favor, creating problems as some women have voiced issues with not finding men "on their level." Yet without acknowledging her advantages, the dismissal of Black men due to status is skewed due to an often unobserved entitlement or unearned sense of social superiority in the public space (especially in media and education) among many Black women.

Black female entitlement could be seen in the split between Black males' earning capacity and Black women's decreasing need for them due to state and philanthropic economic replacement. Termed "Moynihan's scissors" after the despised former assistant secretary of labor in the Johnson Administration, Patrick Moynihan. Reviled by many Black intellectuals, Moynihan is often reduced to blaming Black women for the fall of the Black family due to single-parent parenthood and stating that "the Black family's out-of-wedlock birth rate (then around 25 percent) would soon produce all sorts of progress-halting social ills" (Raspberry, 1995). Despite the accusations, Moynihan also observed a phenomenon few acknowledged:

> [Moynihan's] focus was the jobless rates of nonwhite [Black] males (age 20 and over) and the marital separation rate of nonwhite [Black] females.
>
> Year after year, the lines tracked each other. When joblessness fell between 1952 and 1954, so did the number of women living apart from their husbands; when unemployment surged around 1955, and again in 1958, so did marital separation.
>
> And then something completely unexpected cropped up. Sometime in the early 1960s, the correlation grew weaker until 1963, then it evaporated. The erstwhile parallel lines of [Black] unemployment and [Black] marital separation actually crossed one another—the separation rate moving upward while the jobless rate moved sharply down.
>
> And to this day, Moynihan says he doesn't know why—or what, precisely, it means. Nor does James Q. Wilson who, fascinated, dubbed the crossed lines "Moynihan's Scissors."
>
> (Raspberry, 1995)

Put differently, most other racial groups experienced increases in marital rates the more men were employed. For the Black community, this was reversed. Marital rates declined regardless of Black men's employment a couple of decades after Black women started benefitting from the *man-in-the-house* rule. It could be argued that this entitled sense of intraracial gender superiority was not only rooted in resources that provided Black women independence from the need for men but may have been the source of the heightened resentment toward men who could not provide parity without institutional support.

## V. The End of Black Relationships?

The breakdown between Black men and women has handicapped many ideologies of liberation, integration, and autonomy for the Black community. Put another way, any ideology for advancing the African American community depends on the foundational relationship between Black men and women. The family itself is the foundation of any nationalistic endeavor, as it also is in a democracy. With that institution in disarray, no solution can work. Whether one is a Democrat, a Republican, a Black Nationalist, a Muslim, a Christian, etc., every solution for community uplift is predicated on the Black family. If the family has become unstable, so are any plans based on it. This is what makes the Black gender cold war and the weaponization of the Black family against Black men that much more impactful than other forms of divide and conquer used against the Black community.

This is the unexplored aspect of the Black struggle—not just the decline of the Black family, conveniently occurring after the Civil Rights Movement and during the Black Power era, but the weaponization of the family (and one's love for them) against Black men. Empowered by birth control and family court practices, women hold most of the power regarding family production, divorce, child custody, and child support judgments. Beyond sex and impregnation (whether intentional or not), men have little decision-making power about any of these elements. As such, Black women are more often in positions of authority over the family and in many ways determine the family's perspective regarding Black men.

Black women have been targeted to serve as a Trojan horse of sorts, seduced with buffer-class access designed to undermine stable relationships and Black family formation. By having access to resources that force average Black men to compete with government(s) and institutions to offer women relationship stability, long-term intimate unions are harder to form against bourgeois mating standards. As many cannot, this serves to embolden a sort of entitlement in some, a general superiority complex (e.g., "Black girl magic), while simultaneously developing a sense of Black male inferiority because men cannot seem to achieve what women can on as wide a scale. From this vantage point, the achievements of Black men despite structural pushback become less appreciated when compared to stereotype.

Such destabilizing tactics have utilized policy to entrench successive, multigenerational worldviews of Black male lack. As a result, many generations of Black families perceive Black male failure as a cumulative process, where Black men's incapability to provide ongoing familial stability and economic security becomes how he is pathologized, and the structural aspect of his experience is more and more downplayed. Black women's "new" access to middle-class status seems to help, but these new worldviews of Black male resentment separate Black men and women further. Sadly, it has not taken much material wealth to achieve this split, as Black men and Black women remain in relative poverty compared to other groups. Here, the mere idea of Black female middle-classness is almost enough for many Black women to see themselves as a distinct group separate from Black men. Link this to the academic push to center Black women when blackness is studied—accompanied by the 20,000+ more Black women instructors in the academy—and you have a recipe for Black social, familial, and communal implosion (what this text terms "the Black gender cold war").

It is essential to notice how everything from greater graduation numbers in high school and college; superior faculty hire positions; enhanced access to white-collar employment; an inherited sense of a more accomplished class stratum; a feminism more about Black female advancement than gender equality; and more-targeted educational, employment, family well-being, and organizational investment in Black female advancement than male are all based on policy and not necessarily personal achievement. And if achievement can be legislated by policy, what then of social failure? Can it too be legislated? What about Black males' inability to "keep up" with their Black female counterparts across multiple measures of social standing? Starting in elementary school, Black girls are doing better in mostly female-run schools, being sent to detention and expelled in fewer numbers, being sent to special education in fewer numbers, and graduating and going to college in greater numbers.

This is merely the early stage of the *promotion/demotion thesis*, and it is not a coincidence that the loudest community on issues of American inequality and white supremacy is also the one that is crippled to such a great degree a mere decade after the Civil Rights Movement. Such crippling of the Black community is a product of a range of policies not limited to conscription (or the Selective Service System), where a female-excused war drafting policy exposed generations of Black men to post-traumatic stress disorder, drug use, biochemical warfare fallout, and absence from families (just to name a few) across several major wars.

Another debilitating policy has been gynocentric family court policies (alongside the previously mentioned *man-in-the-house rules)* that laud no-fault divorce, allowing women to divorce husbands arbitrarily. This is devastating for Black men when accompanied by Black women receiving the dominant number of judgments that include child custody, child support, and alimony. This has turned marriage into a trap door to be pulled on men with a one-way drawback (men could not use this same tactic against women and assume they would get the resources women could) that more often underdeveloped men than women as far as the legislation of the decline of the Black nuclear family structure is concerned.

## VI. Birth Control for Me But None for Thee

The widespread access to abortions and the birth control pill since the 1960s (with no equally accessible reproductive pharmaceutical technology for men) further offset familial reproduction. Women now controlled pregnancy far more precisely than in the past. What was once a flip of the coin after sex as to whether a woman was pregnant now became a choice she could make depending on her feelings about a given individual. Women had access to the combination pill, progestin-only pill, female sterilization (including tubal ligation, bilateral salpingectomy, hysterectomy, and transluminal procedures), female condoms, copper IUD, hormonal IUD, patch, vaginal ring, "MPA" shot (depot medroxyprogesterone acetate [DMPA] in injectable form and sold under the brand name Depo-Provera), implant, diaphragm, spermicide, sponges, cervical caps, foams, suppositories, fertility awareness methods, lactational amenorrhea method (breastfeeding as birth control), and the intrauterine system. And none of that included using abortion as a form of birth control. We know that much of this technology came at the expense of many Black women historically in terms of gynecological experimentation and forced sterilization. Still, few discuss the impact this technology had on Black family formation and who has the means to control it from the latter half of the 20th to the first quarter of the 21st century.

Men on the other hand were left with just the pull-out method, vasectomy, and condoms. By comparison, men still use sticks and rocks while women use nuclear technology. This bifurcated approach to birth control gave women an inordinate amount of power to determine their reproductive options while men had to cross their fingers after sex. Couple this pharmaceutical difference with no policies for mandatory DNA testing at birth and no option to opt out of unwanted pregnancies, and men are held hostage to anyone they have sex with or have been sexually violated by, including through dubious and manipulative means (such as coercion or being "forced to penetrate"). This almost single-handedly weaponized men's sexuality against them as far as heterosexual (especially recreational) sex is concerned. However, the accessibility to these pharmaceutical options was legislated by policy, and Black men benefitted little from the aforementioned. In contrast, women benefitted from an unprecedented amount of it. This alone changed Black family formation indefinitely in ways women would never voluntarily relinquish. That said, many Black men began a silent protest, withdrawing their voluntary participation in traditional family formation since the 1960s. Although I argue this is a silent protest, because they saw no other way to address it, this author argues that Black men were forced out of the family through policies that overarchingly advantaged Black women to their detriment.

Put into a popular meme online, men are starting to respond to the weaponization of reproductive options.

*Women:* Can choose to not be a mother during pregnancy, regardless of what is best for the child.
*Men:* Cannot choose.
*Women:* Can choose to abort, and to suggest that she keep it in her pants is offensive.

*Men:* Cannot choose.
*Women:* Can choose to give the child to the state and let the state subsidize this choice.
*Men:* Cannot choose.
*Women:* Can choose to change your mind, and under the safe haven law, and drop her baby off no questions asked.
*Men:* Cannot choose.
*Women:* Can expect to stay to force the male partner to subsidize her choice if she chooses to raise a child.
*Men:* Cannot choose.
*Women:* Can expect to be subsidized by the other parent, even if that other parent is proven not to be the biological parent, because this is in the best interest of the child.
*Men:* Suck it up and pay up. (Author unknown)

## VII. Racialized Gender Access to Education

Title IX is often celebrated for legislating equal opportunity across sex and dampening sexual discrimination. Still, despite its gender-neutral language, the practice of Title IX policies has often overlooked males altogether—especially Black males. Rarely is Title IX associated with accounting for the history of false accusations of rape against Black men that led to tens of thousands of lynchings, incarcerations, or job losses whether from white, Black, or other groups of women. Nor has Title IX been associated with accounting for how Black men often experience sexual discrimination based on generations-old stereotypes about Black male sexual violence and libidinal primitivity. In other words, when treated like a sexual or violent threat simply because they exist, Title IX is not considered a means for protecting such vulnerable Black men because it is primarily perceived as a resource for women.

Another policy impact is the gynocentric K-12 system that advantages girls and is facilitated by many women teachers across races. From grades to graduation rates, girls routinely outperform boys in K-12. In fact, 75% of Black boys in California do not meet state reading standards (Share, 2017). And,

> Only 12 percent of black fourth-grade boys are proficient in reading, compared with 38 percent of white boys, and only 12 percent of black eighth-grade boys are proficient in math, compared with 44 percent of white boys.
> (Gabriel, 2010)

Although Black girls are only ahead in reading comprehension by about 6% at 18%, the differences between Black boys' and girls' educational experiences can be better perceived in terms of college graduation rates over time (Kunjufu, 2020). Even high school graduation rates differ only slightly despite

Black male rates of expulsion and special education tracking. Where it gets confusing is that, technically, more Black males graduate high school than Black females, but that is mainly due to greater high school equivalency certificates (GEDs) than diplomas. Yet for college, there is a striking difference.

> Among Black students in higher education, women are more likely than men to earn degrees: Black women get 64.1% of bachelor's degrees, 71.5% of master's degrees and 65.9% of doctoral, medical, and dental degrees.
>
> (Fast Facts)

In contrast, "According to the *National Center for Education Statistics*, only 36% of Black male students completed a bachelor's degree within six years" (Hill, 2022).

The best way to examine this is through a multigenerational lens. As shown in Table 1.1, between 1976 through 2019, white women outperform every group in terms of college degree attainment. They are followed by white men, then Black women, then Black men. White women have 4.5 times the number of degrees as Black women, while white men have about 6.9 times the number of degrees as Black men. And while white women have 1.4 times the number of degrees as white men, Black women have roughly twice as many as Black men (List of Current Digest Tables, 2021).

Need-based financial aid is the most common financial aid awarded to US college students. This aid typically includes state and federal grants, institutional grants and scholarships, federal loans, and federal work-study. Policy-wise, even need-based financial aid for college and aid for low-income students (including Pell Grants, which formerly incarcerated Black men could not receive before 2020) have funded a gynocentric K-12 system since the 1990s in a manner that has served as a bifurcated system between the genders (Ong, 2022). Women could go into higher education, but men who had formerly been incarcerated could not, especially after degree-attaining programs in prisons were cut by President Bill Clinton's *Violent Crime Control and Law Enforcement Act of 1994*. Also referred to as the 1994 Crime Bill, it denied Pell Grants to inmates and the formerly incarcerated. This greatly impacted Black men trying to establish themselves after prison. As NPR journalists Elissa Nadworny and Lauren Migaki state,

> The 1994 crime bill signed into law by President Bill Clinton banned people in state and federal prisons from accessing federal Pell Grants to pay for college—part of a broad "get tough on crime" political climate at that time. Before the ban, more than 1,500 prisons offered higher education programs.
>
> Without federal funding, the programs vanished. By 1997, it's estimated that only eight remained, according to an American Enterprise Institute report. Those, and newer ones that sprang up in the early 2000s, relied on private funders for financial and volunteer support.

*Table 1.1* Degrees Conferred by Ethnicity and Sex: Selected Years, 1976–2019

| *Degree* | *White* | *Black* | *Sex* | *Black Male* | *Black Female* | *White Male* | *White Female* |
|---|---|---|---|---|---|---|---|
| Certificates | 3,963,492 | 1,079,011 | Male | | | | |
| | 5,475,849 | 2,032,300 | Female | | | | |
| Associates | 4,100,711 | 666,022 | Male | | | | |
| | 6,055,107 | 1,338,013 | Female | | | | |
| Bachelors | 9,715,977 | 1,064,356 | Male | | | | |
| | 12,148,837 | 1,956,578 | Female | | | | |
| Masters | 3,132,157 | 394,539 | Male | | | | |
| | 4,792,204 | 927,847 | Female | | | | |
| Doctorate | 1,009,812 | 72,087 | Male | | | | |
| | 954,507 | 127,911 | Female | | | | |
| Total | 51,348,653 | 9,658,664 | | 3,276,015 | 6,382,649 | 21,922,149 | 29,426,504 |

*Source:* https://nces.ed.gov/programs/digest/d20/tables/dt20_320.20.asp?current=yes

> But over the past decade, advocates across the political spectrum have pushed to lift the Pell Grant ban, fueled in part by research that shows education is one of the most cost-effective ways to keep people from returning to prison once they're released. One study funded by the U.S. Department of Justice found that the risk of recidivism dropped by nearly 13% when people participated in prison education.
>
> (Nadworny, 2022)

Considering that one in three Black men experience incarceration in their lifetime, while one in ten is actively incarcerated, this dynamic of using Pell Grants punitively created a new era of haves and have-nots, especially at a time in the 1970s when college somewhat determined middle-class access. This process seemed to exclude Black men. This is further exacerbated because most of those exonerated from incarceration due to false imprisonment have been Black men. Prison, then, also becomes a means by which scores of innocent Black men may have been barred from college access due to felonious causes, gentrifying generations of Black women while simultaneously underdeveloping scores of Black men.

Policies such as the female-excused military draft, gynocentric welfare practices, family court practices, birth control practices, Title IX implementation, K-12 pedagogy and curriculum, and financial aid disadvantage the small number of Black males attempting to attend college. These policies share a commonality. They each contribute to the *promotion/demotion thesis* argument, which states that society provided advantages to Black women and girls via policy that simultaneously disadvantaged and undermined Black men and boys. Their gain for each set of policies came at the detriment of Black males, yet the advancement aligned with feminism's promise to Black women that they would experience greater equality on par with men. The issue, however, is that Black men have experienced far more institutional anti-Black misandry than patriarchal privilege. Thus, white feminist notions of gender equality translated to intraracial advantage in the Black community. But more specifically, that advantage served as a Trojan horse for destabilizing and sowing seeds of distrust in Black men and women.

# 2 Defining Black Masculinism and the Black Masculinist Turn

## I. What Is Black Masculinism?

Black Masculinism (BM) is both an intellectual and political movement and an analytical/research tool that centers Black males across age, class, and sexuality and seeks to frame the actual state of male life in measurable terms. Advocating both for Black Male Studies and an organic grassroots movement of Black men reassessing their roles in families, community, and society, we endeavor to empirically contextualize the major pillars that indicate Black males' quality of life such as carceral treatment, criminal and civil sentencing, leading causes of death, health, employment, income, wealth status, education, violence, intimate partner violence/homicide, rape, housing and homelessness, types of labor, political approaches, wealth, family court impact (divorce and child custody), fatherhood, forms of protest, marriage, and the history of institutionally based treatment, which are just beginning points of analysis. I call for BM to highlight Black males' lives beyond society's (and academia's) assumptions, often rooted in stereotypes and based on shorthand information, slanderous media representations, and even personal grudges.

BM doesn't presuppose or assume men's innocence (or benevolent humanity) in any given situation but does seek to outline and highlight men's experiential narratives, ultimately highlighting men's humanity—whether inspirational or problematic. As a research tool, BM can also be used multidisciplinarily to analyze film, art, dance, socio-economic status, literature, politics, social behavior (marriage, family, socialization), and many more areas across various fields.

Some of the theories of analysis that undergird BM are anti-Black misandry, white supremacy, Black gynocracy (Black female patriarchy), the dual economy, targeted socio-economic underdevelopment, subordinate male target hypothesis (via Social Dominance Theory), phallicism, John Henryism, institutional exclusion from wealth development, Black male history, and the strategic and historically based use of controlling images in media to shape public perception. From these areas, we frame and interpret Black male life empirically, and thus shape research questions from such influences.

DOI: 10.4324/9781003409441-3

But more than the specificity of how research questions are formed, this text will also expound on the utility of BM. The concept refers to the usefulness of researching Black males in contexts specific to their experiential narratives, historical backgrounds, and sociological and empirical contexts. It applies key conceptual frameworks and theoretic approaches anchored in contexts where many Black males find themselves. Such frameworks are not added arbitrarily, as such work is not accomplished simply because there are men in the room as it is not about theorizing about everyone. Instead, it is specifically about exploring Black male life. Therefore, even in contexts where there is a majority of men, the assumption that research is inherently masculinist is false, no more than assuming a group of women is inherently "feminist." It requires a commitment to an interrogative method to highlight Black men's experiences—but not necessarily their inherent good. Instead, the focus is not to assume Black men's innocence or moral superiority over others but to prioritize finding clarity about Black men's contexts. And Black Male Studies is the repository for these analyses to create a new approach and means of understanding Black males.

Black men have never responded to Black feminism in any organized manner since its inception, and after roughly 40 years of it, it is time they do. In effect, this text calls for two things: for Black men to develop a more cogent and comprehensive response to their labeling by both white society and Black feminism, and the development of a critical sub-field of study that would allow them to develop the means to do so. In some manner, that field would be Black Male Studies. Some would argue that Black Studies has always been preoccupied with Black males, but this is somewhat of a misnomer. Early demonstrations of the field may have used examples comprising Black males, but this is not the same thing as examining the machinations of Black masculinity, nor is it the same as examining the unique experiences Black males undergo that are separate from Black women and children. Black men are often viewed as a pariah and have been since the beginning of the scramble for Africa. In truth, they were viewed as the primary threat against planned colonization and enslavement. Since then, Black men have been the primary targets behind a racialized assault on people of African descent for centuries. In other words, European men saw them as the primary figures to underdevelop, assault, humiliate, emasculate, and kill to dominate Black communities. Acknowledging this need not diminish anyone else, but it is necessary to understand why Black men's experiences are so different from others.

*Black Masculinism* refers to a methodological means of perception, analysis, and gender performance that critically examines historical definitions and representations of Black masculinities, highlighting more progressive alternatives for practical consideration when appropriate but contextualizing past performances against history, socio-economic realities, and Black men's experiences. The concept urges practitioners to articulate the Black male experience as raced, sexed, classed, and gendered (e.g., "Black," "hetero/homo/

GBIT," "working-class/middle-class/upper-middle-class," and "male/masculine"). Furthermore, it purports to develop scholarship that supports the Black community while challenging white supremacy by redefining masculinity (tying it to Black community well-being) and positing progressive gender practices indigenous to Black males' historical experiences rather than anterior to them. Alongside defining new terminology relevant to Black male experiences, BM uses experiential narratives to help us better understand Black male behaviors and circumstances while helping boys and men understand they have a variety of masculinities from which to choose.

*Experiential narratives* refer to a series of narrativized historical nodal points that posit an over-arching Black male experience across contexts. Lastly, the concept seeks to inspire people, especially Black males, to challenge conventional and dehumanizing masculinities and institutionalized white patriarchies to establish their own Black masculinities independent of popular perceptions.

As defined by feminists, *progressive masculinity* generally refers to a practice that challenges gendered, androcentric, patriarchal domination systems. Yet progressive masculinity as defined by Black masculinists suggests that dominating others has not been a central feature of Black masculinity. In fact, it often has not been, historically, for shifting demographic populations of differently configured Black men (based on color, political orientation, religious/spiritual beliefs, gender, sexuality, class, height, voice tenor, etc.). Examples such as W.E.B. DuBois, Robert F. Williams, and Huey P. Newton demonstrate organizational progressivism. In contrast, scores of fathers, brothers, lovers, grandfathers, uncles, boyfriends, etc. demonstrate Black male progressivism daily without fanfare.

It is hoped that through BM, masculinity can be redefined outside of the narrow binary of emasculation and hypermasculinity. It is hoped that via the concept one might recognize myriad opportunities to engage micro- and macro-opportunities to diversify Black male expressive possibilities while not overly shaming those who choose more traditional forms of expression. This liberatory gesture helps create new standards and definitions of gender performance that diversify how Black males of all ages might engage in situations anew. Therefore, at its core, BM is a balancing gesture designed to help develop an appreciation for the subtleties and nuances of Black male lived realities. It is hoped that such a balanced introduction to gender might create mutual gender empathy between Black males and females and a new sense of gender equity through a deep understanding of the Black gender role struggle.

The method for creating such balance via BM is to ground Black men's experiences by filtering them through empirical data, seeking to understand Black male experiences outside stereotypical and mythical tropes. From this standpoint, we can theorize from a research-based position and develop concepts targeted at Black males of varied persuasions in varied contexts. Thus, how might one theorize about poor Black males living within a gynocratic family structure? Or performing subservient expressions of manhood in a traditionally patriarchal space? Or assessing the motivations of a heterosexual Black male wooing a middle-to-upper-class woman? In other words, the concept lends itself to various research possibilities, allowing one to write a Black masculinist review of a theatrical performance, a piece of art, or a philosophical concept by simply relating them to Black males' experiential narratives, historical experiences, and social practices.

Conceived as a counterpart to a "Hudson-Weemsian" Africana womanism(s) (and feminisms that perceive Black males from an empirical basis as opposed to a perspective rooted in stereotype), BM proposes that Black males are profoundly misunderstood, whether by gender studies, Women's Studies, Africana/Black Studies experts, Black scholars, or by many day-to-day Black males themselves (Hudson-Weems, 2019). Black males have been subject to stereotypes taken as truths to the degree that many professional scholars refuse to research and debunk these stereotypes to get to any measurable truth. Whether assumed to be hyper-violent criminals due to popular films, hyper-masculine thugs due to Hip-Hop, or hyper-rapists due to news media, Black males are often not put into context with accuracy, as their misrepresentation often helps other demographics define their own victimization at the expense of Black males.

BM questions the notion of *intersectionality theory*, which initially proposed that Black males were hampered by race but privileged by gender. Instead, the concept suggests there are shifting issues that can denigrate a group while another can further denigrate them in an unforeseen manner. So although Black masculinity is assumed to privilege Black men by feminists, it can also further oppress them, since Black males have not historically been regarded as "men" in the Western sense, hence the relevance of more nuanced theories such as Athena Mutua's *multidimensionality theory* (Mutua, 2013). Black Masculinists invoke dimensions of Mutua's concept in that it posits spheres of empowerment and agency where in some instances heterosexual Black males are in positions of power and where in others Black women, girls, LGBTs, etc. hold power. In other words, the issue is not whether Black males or females lead, but that both (and many more) have led in specific contexts that shift over time. Also, in Mutua's assessment, group interactions cannot be dissected along just one dimension (such as gender) without overlooking other relevant factors. Still, despite the nuance of multidimensionality, Mutua still uses language that posits Black male privilege, despite not defining it empirically, leading to a necessary albeit slight shift by Black masculinists on the nature of multidimensionality. As Dr. Tommy Curry states,

> Even Mutua's rejection of intersectionality has not yet come to grips with the full force of Darren Hutchinson's argument. Despite her concession that there is no empirical evidence for Black men having any "male privileges," Mutua still feels compelled to entertain the notion that there are nebulous privileges attached to Black men. This is an ideological claim

> that remains intuitive for Mutua regardless of fact. This is why the call for a new study of Black men by Black men (similar to my work on genre studies) is necessary to re-situate and historicize Black masculinity beyond pathology and (academic) profit.
>
> (Curry, 2015)

Furthermore, Black Masculinists argue that patriarchy is not universal, especially among Black males. When it has been practiced (or at least seemingly lauded), it has been done so with, often, a form of selectively affirmed consent from Black women when useful in contexts that suited their interests. A brief example can be found in Steve Estes' text *I Am A Man!: Race, Manhood, and the Civil Rights Movement* (Estes, 2006), in which he outlines the various ways post-enslavement Black masculinity seemingly conformed to Western standards to adapt in society. However, mimicking white male patriarchy was not the goal, as Black females and males negotiated their newfound gender dynamics together, something not done in traditional Western patriarchal practice.

## II. What Is the Black Masculinist Turn?

As stated earlier, BM is both a movement and an analytical tool. As a burgeoning "political" movement, it is at the stage where Black males have been exchanging ideas and reflections on Black male life in two major spaces for the last ten years: the academy and online. In the academy, scholars such as myself, Tommy J. Curry, Ronald Neal, William A. Smith, Leamon Bazil, and many others have been publishing in the developing field to carve a new method for analyzing and articulating Black male life. We have been developing new terminology to analyze our experiences better while researching the archives to excavate past scholarship on Black men and boys (research from W.E.B. DuBois, Robert Staples, Bobby Wright, Ishmael Reed, and Darren Hutchinson just to name a few).

Online, especially in social media, Black males have organically begun to meet and compare notes on their experiences in relationships, law enforcement (especially regarding police brutality), family court, and many other areas. This collection of men over the last decade has informally established media channels across YouTube, Twitter, Facebook, Instagram, and several other platforms to draw more Black men to reflect on their various takes on Black male life. These men traverse age, as they range from pre-teens to the elderly, while their geographical location ranges from the U.S. to Africa, to Europe, to Australia, to Asia. In terms of class, they range from the homeless to eight-figure income earners. Their occupations range from those not looking for work to the unemployed to corporate elites. They range from active military to civilians. Their education (from personal interactions with them) ranges from middle school to college professors and scientists. Politically, their philosophies range from Black revolutionary to Black ultra-conservative. Religion runs the gamut of the African diaspora experience: Muslims, Christians, Hebrews, atheists, and traditional African religious practitioners (i.e., Yoruba). Lastly, some live with family, some are married, some are single and range from monks who avoid women to men who have several or who see themselves as lifelong bachelors. It's the widest cross-section of Black men imaginable.

These men have been contemplating their roles as Black men and examining everything from society's expectations of them, the Black community's expectations of them, and their expectations of themselves. They have fiercely debated every topic imaginable, as Black men have not ever had a public stage to do so. But what does this have to do with a "Black Masculinist Turn"?

The Black Masculinist Turn is a moment of pause and reconsideration on Black men's part when encountering brazen, intraracial, anti-Black misandry. It is an acknowledgment—even when it cannot be fully articulated—that the role expected of them is to their detriment far more than to their benefit. They observe that this misandry is specifically targeted toward them and is aggressive. It doesn't meet any of the expectations of any political ideology designed to uplift and improve the quality of the Black community. This hostile, anti-Black misandry is a unique feature that, although seemingly new, goes back generations. The question many of these Black men face is: What exactly should they do about it? It manifests itself in day-to-day behavior, in a hostile media that is anti-male in many respects, and in new political endeavors that ignore the status of Black men and boys. But even within families, when Black male vulnerability is considered, Black boys and men are expected to be sacrificial figures who are only expected to provide but are not necessarily targeted to receive in any impactful way.

When assessing the Black Masculinist Turn, one must know it has three components:"pre-turns," "micro-turns," and "macro-turns." Each of these "turns" allows us to see the various levels to which Black men experience misandric injury within their own families and communities, as well as the larger society.

### *Black Masculinist Pre-Turns*

Black Masculinist Pre-Turns are moments of reflection on phenomena that can go back decades. They refer to historical situations and occurrences shaping social dynamics regarding Black men observing their exploitation and mistreatment. Although this list is not exhaustive, we will provide a few examples of events and occasions that gave many Black men pause at such things as Oprah Winfrey's brand of feminism as seen in her talk show, filmmaking career (most especially *The Color Purple* (Walker, 1985), and her television channel Oprah Winfrey Network (OWN). It either ignored Black men's experiences or castigated them—and Terry McMillan-made films such as *Waiting to Exhale* (Whitaker, 1996) followed suit. Or the 1980s through 1990s television talk show era and its problematic representation of Black men. Or the rise of Kimberle Crenshaw's notion of intersectionality and the subsequent assumption of Black male privilege made on gendered grounds despite a lack of empirical evidence. Or the rise of Black feminism in the 1970s and 1980s that saw Black men as a detriment to Black women much the same way white women and men were. Or the bifurcated access to public aid and regular employment and the subsequent assumptions about men who could not offer women the same level of security they already enjoyed due to said aid. Or the way in which institutions such as the academy, the non-profit sector, aspects of state and federal government, and philanthropic organizations have invested in Black feminist enterprises while ignoring the Black male plight altogether. The tensions surrounding these issues alone remain palpable to this day.

One counterintuitive aspect of Black feminism's relationship to the academy is the degree to which it, and some Black women, seem to be accepted into the mainstream. This goes against all narratives about racism and white supremacy, yet the reality marks how differently Black men and women experience daily reality. With the rise of Kimberly Crenshaw's notion of intersectionality (1989), we saw white liberal academics positively receive intersectionality (and eventually use it as a measure of corporate diversity) while all but removing Black women from its conceptual framework. Still, Black women's advancement of feminism into Africana Studies has been key to downplaying Black men's attempts at an academic, gender-based self-reflection, and more to the point has been hostile to it. Many such men in the academy have learned to either accept the status quo argument that Black women are the most oppressed demographic or operate in silence for fear of being fired. Many Black men have even contacted me to express their concerns about what could happen to their careers, especially if they are caught publicly voicing that they take issue with popular Black feminist approaches to the field of Africana Studies itself, alongside any attempt to define sexuality on terms not directly influenced by feminism. Such institutional hostility and the means used to implement it to shape Black men's academic worldview reveal how much white liberal feminism has institutionally empowered many Black women to serve as gatekeepers in the ghettoized academic environment to which many Black scholars, students, and administrators have been relegated.

Strangely, enough warnings about these power dynamics have come from many places. Comedian Eddie Murphy's comedy stand-up movie, *Raw* (1994), was a *Black Masculinist Pre-Turn*. Murphy's warnings to Black men (and men in general) about divorce and the debilitating impact of losing half of what you have simply based on her whims, indicated to men that our vulnerability in the eyes of the family court was irrelevant. His sometimes crass yet poignant reflections on dating internationally even played out nearly 30 years later as many Black men are now reflecting on the problems with bringing foreign wives back to the United States and having Black women, family members, and friends be the first to initiate them into the gynopotestal framework—as Murphy joked, to tell foreign women that they should not engage Black men on traditional terms in marriages but only on the terms they, Black women, were comfortable with. So even Murphy's performance reflects how a 1990s-era comedy helped inform Black men about intraracial, anti-Black misandry.

But songs on the radio, too, caused concern. Songs such as Erykah Badu's "Tyrone" (1997) or TLC's "No Scrubs" (1999) and the subsequent celebration that went along with these performances in private spaces, events, concerts, recordings, clubs, classrooms, and their general reception in both the Black community and the larger public caused many Black men to pause and observe how they were perceived and treated within their own communities.

### *Black Masculinist Micro-Turns*

*Black Masculinist Micro-Turns* are smaller in scale or constitute small-scale events, but nonetheless impact Black families and communities through media productions and public events. A key marker to them is that they deeply impact individual men personally through family and social dynamics.

For example, there has been a recent slew of online Black women therapists who have presented themselves in social media from 2020 to 2023 and openly advocated not treating Black men, downplaying Black male issues, and promoting the overall perspective that Black men were not worth addressing, were considered less than human, and were justified in being ignored. This is particularly problematic as psychology is, according to economist Richard Reeves, becoming increasingly a field solely occupied by women. As the rates move closer to an all-female field of study, how counselors and psychologists are trained regarding men may move more to speculation on a group in abstraction than based on something shaped in concert with men. Such speculation could offset whole generations of therapists on men's humanity, much the way the Duluth Model can be said to have unduly manipulated generations of scholarship on abuse and sexual assault. Considered a product of patriarchy alone, the Duluth Model became a broad sword that castigated men as the source of sexist violence, making them incapable of being victims (Curry, 2017). This helped make society incapable of perceiving women's capacity for violence independent of men.

Another micro-turn that goes back decades is the divorce rate in the United States. Extremely high in Black America most especially, Black women are both the most divorced and the least married, a difficult challenge for Black men who want to marry Black women. Fifty-one percent of marriages end in divorce, and second and third marriages have much higher rates. Added to divorce stories, family court judgments regarding child support and alimony pressure men to step back from marriage. The automatic gesture of extending women's custody over using a case-by-case method where the parent best suited should get primary custody has become a problem that the courts have not yet fully recognized. Additionally, the idea that women could divorce husbands at any time and get child support and/or alimony to supplement their lifestyle makes marriage dangerous for the average man. And a man could find himself vulnerable to multiple divorces and debt for years.

Another micro-turn can be observed in social media. In conversations on YouTube, Twitter, and on apps such as Clubhouse, Black women "divestors" (women who refuse to date, marry, or associate with Black men) gather to talk about Black men's inherent inferiority to white men and how Black men do not deserve to live. Terms such as "bullet bags" have frequently framed Black men as inhuman animals only worthy of death. Such practices are becoming such a regular occurrence in social media spaces that many Black men have been reflecting on how deeply these perspectives are held by many of the Black women they know.

In response to this, and to the low-boiling contempt many Black men feel from Black women, most recently a new group of men has been introduced to mainstream culture via social media. They called themselves *#PassportBros* and have entirely opted out of relationships with Western women. Passport "bros" are mostly American Black men who have decided to exercise their mating choice options and find intimate, social, and marital relationships with women from other cultures. They are, essentially, on strike. Ironically, despite the contempt some have directed at *#PassportBros*, such has already been done decades before by Black women themselves. In 1996, author Terry McMillan wrote *How Stella Got Her Groove Back*, a book made into a film two years later. This spawned a low-key movement amongst educated, white-collared, Black women to travel internationally for men perceived as a more viable option than American Black men. The story visages a 40-something, highly successful corporate Black woman who runs out of dating options in America. She goes to Jamaica to meet up with a young, viral, muscular, young man whose life and career experience are far beneath her own. The idea is that American Black men are no longer viable; thus, women have to go elsewhere to find viable partners. For the most part, Black men at the time did not oppose these messages entirely. The most they did was opt out of watching such films or reading such books, but more Black women began to travel and talk about dating "out" in various ways. By 2022, when Black men started talking about doing the same thing, they were accused of everything from being disloyal to being exploitive of women, and some even went so far as to accuse these men of being pedophiles—despite the fact that age had not been a major factor in their motivations for travel. Such a backlash against this small group began another pause for Black men. Another Black Masculinist Turn. Men who do not even consider themselves passport bros took a deep interest in how much animosity was directed at them and not at Black women since the 1990s who decided to travel abroad to find young Black men (or men of other races) to occupy their time and interest. (Interestingly, Eddie Murphy also joked about this in *Raw* when discussing Black women traveling to Jamaica for sex.)

Another micro-turn has been the Black gynopotestal family itself. As stated before, such a family dynamic sees men as replaceable, disposable tools to be used, exchanged, or discarded when convenient. These men are not seen as much more than utilities and are associated with a specific type of sexual objectification we avoid discussing as it relates to heterosexual men. These men are exploited because they are heterosexual (as Black women seldom seek out gay men for marriage, reproduction, and sex), Black, and male. They are perceived yet again to be not more than resources or steppingstones to advantage women who are perceived to be, as far as the Black community is concerned, the only viable options for familial, communal, and political leadership. Black gynopotestal families prioritize their girls' education and career while telling the boys they need to work. This is the basis of the gynopotestal family, as each woman is expected to be the head of her respective household, so it is required that she have the requisite education and work experience to be such. Reflection on gender roles in the Black community has caused many Black men in the last ten years to re-examine their position in families, relationships, and community. Many find that they are not respected and come from family lines of men who have also not been respected.

### *Black Masculinist Macro-Turns*

*Black Masculinist Macro-Turns* are the basis for the idea of turns. I first encountered this concept after reflecting upon how a certain man's death was received publicly. From there I worked retroactively to find a pattern. Quite coincidentally, I also found a pattern of men awestruck by the audacity of such brazen misandry that it left many in silence. These men began to reach out, send messages, and create content online in an attempt to come to grips with what they were witnessing, but they often not did not have the language to do so. The pure and sheer animosity many men faced (animosity that started about other issues but quickly became about them) was palpable.

The man whose death sparked this observation was Kevin Samuels, an image consultant and YouTube content creator who became controversially popular in 2021. He garnered over 1 million subscribers in record time by giving dating advice based on the concept of sexual marketplace value, the idea that people have varying degrees of social value in the social dating marketplace (their degree of attractiveness) based on age, bodily aesthetics, resources, status, and other such qualifiers. He argued that one's sexual attractiveness had much to do with whether one meets the desires of the opposite sex (obviously the concept fixated on heterosexual dynamics). Based on online influencer Rollo Tomassi's concept, the idea of sexual marketplace value was such that younger women and older men's interests dominated the marketplace (Tomassi, 2013). In other words, younger women were most sought after because men (for the most part) valued their youth and beauty. In contrast, older men were considered the most desirable by women because of their status and capacity to attain resources.

Nightly, people (mostly Black women) would call Samuels' show on YouTube, and he would assess their status against marketplace values. He often framed "high value" Black men and their accomplishments as rare, which had not been traditionally done, especially in public media. Based on such rarity, he identified them as being sought after by most women (across races) and proved it almost nightly when woman after woman would articulate what she wanted in an ideal man. Most women called in about men who ranked in the top 10%. This meant that they earned six figures, were over 6 feet tall, owned a home, owned a car, were physically fit, and had a successful business or career. In popular culture, these men are perceived as being in ample supply. Samuels, however, argued they were quite rare, and thus, because of their rarity could command a higher price in the sexual dating marketplace. Put differently, their status allows them to seek out more desirable women and prioritize sexual needs and interests. Samuels suggested changing weight, fitness, and income to meet the opposite sex's interests for both genders, challenging longstanding practices of pedestalizing women and negatively blaming men for the current state of the dating market. This was the norm in the dating coach world, and many women have grown quite accustomed to it. Celebrity relationship gurus such as Steve Harvey and Iyanla Van Zant argued for decades that when it came to Black dating, Black men needed to cater to women's desires and to be seductive, wealthy, fit, handsome, etc. Women, on the other hand, did not have such parameters and were expected to be accepted however they presented themselves to men. Any critique of such an approach was seen as misogynistic. Yet the brazen misandry of requiring men to meet popular culture's standards for women (often based on income) has not been sufficiently challenged—that is, until Kevin Samuels.

Samuels overturned that dynamic and created a very complicated relationship with the public. In some respects, his viewing numbers would exceed large networks such as NBC and CNN. Nightly, women (mostly Black women) would call in large numbers to ask for advice while arguing with him or being hurt by what he said. Some of his videos went viral on social media from Twitter to WorldStarHipHop, and the sensationalism of the arguments that took place often distracted people from the deeper message. The deeper message was simply that in human social dynamics, relationships require a cost commensurate with whatever outcome one desires. The caveat to that seemingly commonsense argument is that in the Black community, it has mainly been Black men who were told they needed to qualify for women's interests, not the reverse. But the other aspect of the deeper message was that Samuels wanted Black families via marriage over single parenthood. He pushed for Black coupling on the basis that both Black men and women accept their actual sexual marketplace value (void of fantastical self-aggrandizement) and engage people who matched their status. He urged that people engage in therapy and put aside fantasy to take relationships more seriously while still young enough to have children. But, if one wanted to date above their "station," they must meet the desires of those who operate at such stations instead of assuming that people should just accept whatever they decide they want others to value.

On May 5, 2022, Samuels suffered from hypertension and passed away. The news hit social media within a couple of hours of his passing. Soon after, some Black women celebrated his passing with parties, others laughed in videos and suggested it was karma, while others proclaimed that God (or "Goddess") came down and punished him. Some men were so disgusted by these displays they left social media. And more than a few different types of men, regardless of their attitudes about Kevin Samuels directly, were shocked at the level of vitriol these women expressed toward Samuels. More to the point, it did not take long until conversations about him became about Black men, many of whom had little to do with Samuels. Some of them had not even heard of Samuels, yet somehow, they still became repositors of women's rage, which existed long before his passing.

Some pontificated that the rage toward Black men in the dating market had to do with the idea that there were too few of them and that not enough met this fantastical standard that many Black women had developed since the 1980s. When Black women began celebrating their newfound careerism, the standards for how well-qualified men were defined increased dramatically. This meant that men who decades before (as it relates to one's grandparents for example) would have been viable spouses were no longer such by today's standards. Average Black men are often not considered good enough for average women based on many publicly stated articulations of ideal manhood.

By the standards of today's media-influenced Western women, viable male candidates are expected to be within the top 3 to 10% of men on multiple axes. At least since the 1980s, many women have wanted a man with a 9 to 12-inch penis, a six-figure income, a college degree, a fit and muscular physique, and a height of over 6' 2". This is particularly interesting considering how easily such numbers get into the single-digit realm. For example, only about 2% of the population can bench press over 225 pounds (Luna, 2023). Only 3.9% of the male human population is over 6' 2" (Ly, 1996). Around 10% of Black folk earn over $89,000 yearly by household and before taxes, and only 5% make more than $112,000 yearly (Noël, 2014). Half as many Black men have gotten degrees as Black women since 1976 (and there has not been a year where Black men have gotten more degrees than Black women). And according to a 2014 study, the "average size for an erect penis is 14.2 cm (5.6 inches)" (MacGill, 2022). Putting such standards on Black men is ridiculous but has become nonetheless normalized, as this is what "produced" Samuels in the first place. As much as he was reviled as a misogynist, most ignore that he was a direct response to Black women's stated desires since the

1980s. Either way, Black men are frustratingly responding to these unrealistic desires, disrupting the dating marketplace due to the Black Masculinist Turn against the celebratory response to Kevin Samuels' death.

O'Shea Jackson's, or Ice Cube's, visit to Fox Soul's online show *Cocktails With Queens* with Black women celebrities Claudia Jordan, LisaRaye McCoy, Vivica A. Fox, and Syleena Johnson was probably just as impactful. In that show he was interviewed by several of the celebrity Black female hosts about his plan Contract With Black America, which he presented to both candidates in the presidential race in 2020. H was willing to sit down with Republicans or Democrats based on the argument that neither has truly benefited Black America. To many in the Black community, one party has historically ignored Black America. At the same time, the other exploits us with unfulfilled promises to increase access to jobs, resources, and business investments. Upon going on the show, however, he received hostility and indignation from the hosts because he did not provide a specific plan for Black women, even though he did not provide a specific plan for any gender (men included). His plan was communal in focus, but the women were frustrated that he did nothing for Black women specifically in his proposal. He even invited them to help him write it.

Nevertheless, the vitriol and hostility not only by the women on the panel but also by women in the comments were such that it served as another macro-turn. Meaning, Black men stood in awe at the brazen misandry of the hostility to Ice Cube and Black men. Black women, on the other hand, have developed their own vocabulary and their own political interest since the 1980s (some could even argue since the 1970s). Black women can talk about policies, grants, and resources that should be targeted specifically to Black women and girls for social advancement. Even mothers of sons still talk about advancing female-only priorities. This bifurcated relationship between Black men and women in politics came to a head in Ice Cube's discussion on *Cocktails With Queens* and in so doing caused a subtle rift between many Black men and women. It was a rift that men would only grumble about under their breath, but based on the commentary of seething frustration amongst many Black men, this is where you started to see a major change. For the first time in decades, Black men began to slowly articulate their concerns and their ire at being dismissed in this manner.

Another Black Masculinist Macro-Turn could be argued around Black male celebrities falsely accused of sexual assault and rape. One such case was the case of Brian Banks, a high school football star who held a lot of promise regarding the possibility of him going to the NFL. At one point in his high school senior year, he was accused of rape by a fellow classmate. He spent five years in jail, and five years on probation, dashing all his hopes to go to the NFL while the girl who accused him of rape and her family received $1.5 million from the local school system. Years later, after she attempted to reconnect with him on Facebook, he could record her on camera, suggesting that she falsified her accusation. It didn't take long for him to be exonerated of his rape charge and even receive an invitation to play briefly in the NFL. But this Black Masculinist Macro-Turn was not only a blatant case of women using their institutional capacity to accuse Black men of false crimes with no repercussions, but it also became a clear indication that (as men have been saying for years) this was an unchecked power women had. We have no statistics regarding how often it was abused, but posting *#MeToo* gave random women the power to destroy a man's life (*Breaking News Live Media,* 2017). Some were even accusing celebrities who had died years prior of atrocities committed against them decades ago, and again there was no opportunity for men to push back.

Another such false accusation was the case of singer Chris Brown in 2022 (Dillon, 2022). Brown, already hated in some circles because of his physical altercation with the singer Rihanna in 2009, had been demonized in the court of public opinion when this new accusation came forth. Nevertheless, it wasn't long after that Brown was able to produce text messages to prove his innocence and that this young woman fabricated a story. And, much like other false accusations, upon finding out about his innocence, the public has still not apologized to Brown. They merely ignored it and swept it under the rug. Yet again, the woman in question was not punished for her false accusation. She was not even named publicly or shown in the articles about her, as women can make false accusations without repercussions. Their names are not made public. Their faces are not made public. Yet the stain of the accusations on his record revealed a one-sided dynamic seen as acceptable to far too many, but more and more men are starting to take issue with this.

Although white, a major turn in 2022 was the case of Johnny Depp. Depp was accused of sexual assault and abuse by his girlfriend, Amber Heard. However, he was able to record an audio clip of Heard being aggressive, admitting to abusing him. This shocked and split the public because many were familiar with the tropes of women being victimized by men, but very few knew how to empathize with men who were victimized by women. The fact that some women take advantage of this culture of #BelieveAllWomen while knowing a man is less likely to be believed is reprehensible. Heard was caught telling Depp that no one would believe him! So, in 2022 when Johnny Depp won his case in California against Heard, it sent shock waves through the mainstream because it meant there was now a record (alongside Brian Banks) of women being shown abusing the public's trust in them. But what does Depp's case have to do with Black men? It means they serve as the "canaries in the mine" on many an issue. But if a white male celebrity can be exonerated in court, the question is: Will more Black men being falsely accused and imprisoned receive the same treatment? Will the public accept the idea that women can abuse the system? Will the public be willing to extend empathy for Black men, or will they resort to the old tropes of men/bad and women/good?

Similar false charges were levied against former NFL player Michael Irvin and actor Jonathan Majors in 2022. In each case, questions arose about whether the women making these accusations did so in good faith or whether they were exploiting the public's sense of right and wrong. In the case of Irvin, there's video evidence of him having an innocent, short conversation with a hotel worker that later turned into an accusation of impropriety against him. This cost Irvin an opportunity to cohost the 2023 Super Bowl. Companies such as the NFL tend to immediately sever contracts out of fear of being accused of supporting rape culture if they continue to employ people who are falsely accused. A similar thing happened to actor Jonathan Majors when his girlfriend accused him of having physically assaulted her, leading to his arrest, even though he was the one to call the police. Within 24 hours of that arrest, the U.S. Army canceled its contract with him regarding the commercials for which he served as spokesman. But the cancellations of Irvin and Majors in the face of such accusations suggest a culture of believing women at the expense of truth. This is not to say that both men are innocent. We may find out much more by the time this book is published. To date, it suggests that there's enough evidence to cause doubt and allow for discussion, but people quickly assume male guilt because it is familiar.

One of the biggest macro-turns was Black Lives Matter (or BLM), now the Black Lives Matter Global Network Foundation. The organization took the Black activist community, and Black America, by storm because many of us thought it was the next evolution of a longstanding Black protest tradition. However, the first indicator that it was different was the feminist bent the organization took. Its website became well known for setting its sights on the nuclear family and advocating for a family without Black men.

After the death of Michael Brown, however, the approach the organization took was to seek out victimized, Black men and then, while appearing to advocate for them, bait and switch the focus back onto Black women. The organization itself was not welcoming to Black men overall and would not allow Black men to take leadership positions in the group. BLM chapters in different cities found that if led by heterosexual Black men, they were often not well received. In many instances, these chapters would not even be recognized as organization members. Much of this was explained in real time by activist Darren Seals when the organization appropriated funds from the Ferguson movement during conflicts with its own law enforcement agencies.

According to Seals, when the people in Ferguson, Missouri, started to protest police abuse and the killing of Michael Brown, it was not long before activists on Twitter began to migrate to Ferguson. More and more came, but Seals found that many spent most of their time on their phones tweeting about what was happening. Across different social media posts, Seals commented on how many of these people did not seem to have a direct connection to the people of Ferguson. More particularly, he found out they were successfully raising funds online, but most people in Ferguson did not have a Twitter presence. By doing this, white donors began to donate to people who claimed they were part of the Ferguson activist movement but were not. Seals suggested that BLM was also part of this dynamic, as it began to receive resources that should have gone to native Ferguson's Black residents who were the leading push behind the protest. That said, it is unsurprising that a few years later in 2020, BLM would amass about $90 million in organizational donations. In the eyes of some Black men, this was starting to look like the work of vultures eating the carcasses of unjust Black male police homicides. It no longer struck the same tone as past generations of activist organizations attempting to uplift Black America. Instead, it started to feel much more like a new era of activism aimed to exploit Black male death for the political advancement of Black feminist women.

More problematically, Patrisse Cullors, one of the three founding members of BLM, was discovered to have made significant real estate purchases around the same time BLM received this windfall of millions of dollars. Most particularly in Los Angeles, the purchase of a $6 million mansion raised eyebrows within and without the organization. Many BLM chapters grumbled that they had received no support from the primary BLM leadership, despite donating millions of dollars. When BLM leaders did reveal that they would start sending out resources, they primarily only did so for queer, Black, women-led chapters, leaving heterosexual Black male leaders with no resources or support from the primary BLM leadership because their chapters were not recognized. That BLM not only avoided supporting heterosexual Black men but had no problem profiting from that very demographic's deaths raised concern in many Black men. This was not the activism of old.

In the eyes of white America, BLM became synonymous with Black protest, much the same way the NAACP and other similar organizations during the Civil Rights Movement became synonymous with said movement. The problem with this was that the group became known for quickly responding to the deaths of Black men unjustly killed by police or vigilantes but then changing the issue to issues prioritizing Black women, Black intersectional feminism, LGBTQ+ issues, and other such peripheral discussions to that of police homicide in the Black community.

In the public sphere, discussions about whether Black men participated enough or were too cowardly to protest began circulating. This was ironic considering that after the death of Michael Brown, which attracted so many to Ferguson, many Black males were involved. Many were activists and pastors from other places, but others, including Black gang members, were ready to go toe-to-toe with the police. However, they were eventually drowned out by visiting cadre of Black women who were overwhelmingly better educated and better organized. In this way, the situation in Ferguson in 2014 became much like when the *Student Non-Violent Coordinating Committee* (SNCC) invited an influx of better-educated whites to join the organization in the 1960s to stem violence from the police and to attract media coverage of their protests (except Ferguson did not invite this group to support its movement) (Carmichael, 2003). The young white activists were better organizers and planners too. They looked down on the aggressive nature of Black political dissent within SNCC (and resented taking orders from young Black activists). Similarly, this cadre of mostly Black middle-class, young, college-educated women in Ferguson saw this Black male proletariat as impassioned. Still, it misled their desire for violence (many also resented taking leadership from men, having viewed the Civil Rights and Black Power Movements as patriarchal). Yet Akinyele Umoja's "We Will Shoot Back: The Natchez Model and Paramilitary Organization in the Mississippi Freedom Movement" (Umoja, 2014) showed us that violence—even during the Civil Rights Movement—played a key role and served as a check against white conservatism and its rejection of peaceful Black protest. In other words, the threat of Black violence proverbially said, "If you don't accept the non-violent grassroots protest of this mostly Black women-comprised movement, you'll have to deal with the violence from this mostly Black male veteran-led underground movement."

Black men began to have reservations about BLM because of Darren Seals (not counting the Black men who attempted to establish unrecognized BLM chapters or those told they could not lead in the organization because they were hetero-Black males). Black Panther Kathleen Cleaver expertly explains why Black males did not join BLM by describing the differences between BLM and the Black Panther Party (BPP). She argues that the reason that the BPP appealed/s to men is based on a gendered historical set of models. The BPP, created by two men (one a veteran and another a law student) was based on the "warrior"-based, militaristic philosophies of Malcolm X and Ho Chi Minh. In contrast, BLM, started by three Black women activists, is based on the activist, group-consensus leadership model of Ella Baker of SNCC. In this way, they each appealed to models tailored to Black males or females (Detroit Public TV, 2016).

The last Black Masculinist Macro-Turn is political and focuses on Stacey Abrams and Kamala Harris. For Harris, the year of Joe Biden's electoral run came alongside a demand by Black women in the Democrat Party that the next vice president be a Black woman. This was partly meant to reflect the need to represent Black women, since Barack Obama had adequately represented Black men. Some would argue that the problem with this dynamic is that because Barack Obama was not a Black person in America whose lineage descended from those enslaved, the question of whether he could represent the Black male experience is left up for debate. Still, Harris, as problematic a choice as Obama regarding indigeneity (she is of Jamaican and South Asian descent), became the chosen representation for a Black woman at the executive political level. For many Black men, this was a problem because Harris had a record in the California Bay Area for incarcerating Black men. This did not sit well with some Black men as far as which chosen candidate would be picked by Biden's administration.

However, the point raised here regarding the Black Masculinist Turn was that Black women demanded a Black women candidate to be vice president but did not acknowledge Black men's concerns about which candidate should be an option. Much of this came from a notion that Black women have voted for Democrats to unprecedented degrees for decades but did not see themselves represented in the candidates chosen. Although true, what was overlooked was that Black men voted to the second highest degree despite the misnomer that they do not vote. The problem with this assumption is that Black men are the most voter-disenfranchised group. Due to high levels of incarceration, many Black men do not have the right to vote and yet, despite this they tend to vote Democrat to the highest degree—just under Black women, who do not experience voter disenfranchisement anything like Black men. So, removing the Black male presence from any serious discussion about who should be considered a vice-presidential candidate seemed a slight of sorts.

This author argues that even when it pertains to Barack Obama, it is not that Black men voted Barack Obama into office and Black women were ignored. It is that many Black people voted for Barack Obama, but Black women only voted for Barack Obama as a proxy for Michelle Obama. The celebration of the election of President Obama had to do more with (amongst many Black women) to whom he was married. This is not necessarily a reflection of his politics. It reflected which woman would serve as the first lady. Adding that caveat to this discourse, we can observe that the question of whom should serve in which office leaned toward Black women in both contexts—whether it be about the first lady or who should be the first Black vice president, both prioritized Black women.

Stacey Abrams ran for governor of Georgia in 2022. Questions were eventually raised about whether Black men would support her candidacy to a great enough degree for her to get into office. In response, Abrams launched a low-level campaign to secure the Black male vote. She held an hour-long session in Atlanta where she spoke for approximately 30 minutes about the importance of abortion and other issues that did not necessarily speak directly to Black men. She did not even really engage in a back-and-forth conversation with the Black men she invited so that she could plead her case as to why they should vote for her. Instead, she gave a mini-lecture about the important issues of the day, most issues that pertain to Black women, then left. Following this, Black men debated online whether she supported their issues sincerely. In response, she created a "Black Men's Agenda" (Abrams, 2022). Her agenda attempted—solely by using the term "agenda"—to usurp the momentum of the *17-Point Black Male Political Agenda* that this book supports. But the contents of her Black Man's Agenda had no particularity to their needs. Instead, she used generic Democrat-based policies that would benefit anyone who applied for them. She also suggested that because these policies existed, Black men would be supported on that basis alone and did not require policies specific to them. However, after she lost the election, it was revealed that Black men had voted for her, but she still did not win.

The primary issue of Black women in politics is that more of them have been making it into office over the last few decades, primarily due to advanced education. The second reason of note as to why Black women politicians constitute a *Black Masculinist Macro-Turn* is because when the conversation shifted to Black men needing to help elect Black women (and this would include Mayors Lori Lightfoot of Chicago, Karen Bass of Los Angeles, and many others when you include lower-level electoral positions such as judges, aldermen, etc.), it became clear that Black women such as Harris, Abrams, Lightfoot, and Bass had no sense whatsoever of what Black men's political interests were, nor did they demonstrate any significant care that those politics might be different from Black women's ideas about what needed to happen if Black women politicians were successfully elected to enact policy.

After all this, can we now ask whether Black men and boys have different needs than Black women and girls? Should there be separate political agendas? Are there any other differences that have been disregarded over the generations of political mobilization and activism? Can such differences be drawn out without devolving into accusations of misogyny if Black women and girls are not prioritized in every discussion, which seems the accepted status quo related to contemporary intraracial gender discourse?

# 3 Anti-Black Misandry

Black men endure a misunderstood form of sexism that African American philosopher Tommy J. Curry terms 'anti-Black misandry' (ABM). According to him, anti-Black misandry is

> the cumulative assertions of Black male inferiority due to errant psychologies of lack, dispositions of deviance, or hyper-personality traits (e.g., hyper-sexuality, hyper-masculinity) which rationalize the criminalization, phobics, and sanctioning of Black male life. These ideas are part of the group-based racial consciousness of white America and part of the social fabric and mythology of racism.
>
> (Curry, 2018)

Defining ABM in such fashion, Curry links society's misunderstanding of it to the general phobia of Black men et al, white supremacy, and the popularity of negative stereotypes that obscure the realities of male African Americans. Consequently, numerous Black men often remain unaware they have been sexually victimized because they have not been socialized to think of themselves in gendered terms.

Anti-Black misandry plays out in a variety of contexts: pitiable education, low social expectations, extreme wage gap, diminished job access, limited labor choices, poor health, inadequate access to healthcare, heightened incarceration, and social hyper-villainization make Black males the primary recipients of such forms of systemic victimization. However, what is arguably worse is that countless Black males' experience with victimization has been virtually ignored by gender theorists and in popular media.

It is in this sense that the concept of anti-Black misandry is useful. As a conceptual lens for reconsidering Black male life, it can help contextualize the bevy of data on Black males that in the past was relegated strictly to racism. Regarding Black men's victimization because of their gender, the possibility of developing helpful policies increases. Health, policy, incarceration, education, and employment constitute just a few Black male underdevelopment areas requiring crucial reconsideration. In current gender discourses, many

DOI: 10.4324/9781003409441-4

of these areas remain an untouched conceptual domain as numerous Black males' gender experiences are invisible, ignored, and consequently undertheorized, even while their deaths serve as fetishized entertainment for some and fodder for political mobilization for others. Yet the reasons for their deaths remain misunderstood, and the particular breadth of their experiences as raced and gendered beings go disregarded. In this sense, it is acceptable to question whether Black males are truly disposable.

Black men grapple with anti-Black misandry, a form of racialized sexism often confused with racism due to academic and popular media influences. This is further exacerbated by popular gynocentric approaches to gender that malign Black men. The combination of these elements hampers the development of a widespread understanding or movement for opposing ABM. Without a large-scale political movement or a mass media campaign to shed light on the full spectrum of Black male vulnerability, the need to clarify how it functions is much more necessary. To achieve such clarification, it is first necessary to develop at least three things: a new gender vocabulary, a new field titled *Black Male Studies*, and a cultural movement of Black men across all walks of life to better elucidate the nature of institutional misandry in a white patriarchal context. Using empiricism, history, and Black male testimonies as a starting point, we can collectively provide a more useful approach to studying Black males and push to improve their quality of life dramatically.

## I. Anti-Black Misandry

*Anti-Black misandry* is a form of racialized sexism that refers to the hatred of Black males based on both their gender and their race. Put more succinctly, William A. Smith, Tara J. Yosso, and Daniel G. Solórzano argue that "[anti-] Black misandry refers to an exaggerated pathological aversion toward Black men created and reinforced in societal, institutional, and individual ideologies, practices, and behaviors" (Smith et al., 2007). Designed to highlight the sexist treatment of Black males intra-racially, interracially, and extra-racially in both intimate and societal contexts (i.e., incarceration rates, high special ed. rates, high expulsion rates, low graduation rates, high police brutality rates, etc.), the concept highlights a particular hatred for Black males that supersedes social class and sexuality.

Hatred of Black men has been deeply inculcated into the very fabric of American culture, both individually and institutionally. Even in Black America, males and females learn very early that anti-Black misandry is a normalized fixture in the daily doings of many Black folks. Historically, it first manifested in whites' perspective that Black men were childlike and thus had not achieved manhood by the Western standard. In fact, anti-Black misandry stems from several overarching notions of Black masculinity rooted in stereotypes. Since the 18th century, Black men were perceived as effeminate in that they were: not men (i.e., white men), hypermasculine, hyper-violent, hypersexual, limited in intelligence, irrational, and incompetent.

These overarching ideas manifested in the myriad stereotypes made of Black males found in the post-slavery era such as the "Buck," the "Brute," the "Mandingo," the "Sambo," the "Uncle Tom," the "Zip Coon," the "Noble Savage," the "Pimp," the "Player," and the "Gangsta" just to name a few (with some obviously made from the 1970s through the 1990s). Each deviates and falls short of Western (code for white) masculinities in that they are irrational, brutal, exploitive, criminalistic, cowardly, or lack intelligence. Such a brew of assumed ideas has shaped popular perception of Black males over the centuries. In fact, Black males are then incapable of being victims due to their hyper-violent temperament. They then become aggressors, even when victims, and are thus deserving of violence. For example, 54-year-old Craig Adams was shot in front of his home by a police officer for holding a BBQ fork (Savali, 2017). Or soon-to-graduate Army Lt. Richard Collins III, who was killed for no other reason than standing and waiting for an Uber ride (Sacks & Nashrulla, 2017). Or DeShawn Franklin, an 18-year-old Black male who was punched, tasered, and arrested by police while sleeping in his bed (he was later awarded $18 by a jury) (Phillips, 2016). Or 24-year-old Ramad Chatman, a man found 'not guilty' of a crime but still sentenced to seven years in prison (Harriot, 2017). Or 40-year-old Tashii Brown, unarmed yet tasered and choked to death by Las Vegas police officers (Kaleem, 2017).

Black male demagoguery is so acceptable that law enforcement sometimes knowingly incarcerates innocent Black men because society accepts their guilt. In a shocking example, a death-row inmate of 34 years, Kevin Cooper, was "on death row because the San Bernardino Sheriff's Department framed him," the judge, William A. Fletcher of the Ninth Circuit Court of Appeals, declared in a searing 2013 critique delivered in a distinguished lecture series (Kristof, 2017; Fletcher, 2014)." But it's not only a judge who found him innocent; so too did the surviving victim. The survivor,

> a then 8-year-old Josh Ryen . . . had his throat cut and was left for dead. Josh Ryen recovered from his injuries, he stated that it was three white or Hispanic men that attacked and killed his family and that Cooper was not involved. This started a chain of events that now indicate a startling 30 year cover up and blatant falsification of evidence by law enforcement and the prosecutor's office in the case. This includes the fact that the blood at the crime scene did not belong to Cooper and contained the DNA of two people. But now there is no sample left because it was consumed during the testing process.
>
> (Barnes, 2016)

Another example is Clarence Moses-El, a Denver man who was arrested in 1987 and served 28 of a 48-year sentence for a rape he did not commit but was charged for based on the fact that the female victim dreamed he raped her. *The Guardian* states,

> On a summer night in 1987, a Denver woman was out drinking with three men, and after saying goodnight and returning home, was severely beaten and raped in her apartment. Her facial bones were broken and she lost sight in one eye.
>
> The victim first told police it was too dark to identify her attacker, then said it was one of the three men. A day and a half later, she said it came to her in a dream that the assailant was her neighbor, Clarence Moses-El.
>
> (Hesse, 2015)

Even more shockingly,

> Twenty-five years later, convicted rapist L.C. Jackson wrote a letter to Moses-El confessing in December 2013. "I really don't know what to say to you, but let's start by bringing what was done in the dark into the light," Jackson wrote, according to court documents. "I have a lot on my heart." The rape victim initially named Jackson when police questioned her. But Jackson was never arrested and later raped another woman and her daughter in 1992, about a mile and a half away from the first woman's home.
>
> (Ng, 2015)

Moses-El, 60 years old in 2017, spent 28 years in jail without evidence because as a Black man, his guilt was acceptable, even after the real rapist confessed! It fits the view of Black men and was sufficient evidence "just because." These are just a few examples of how, despite innocence (and no arms), Black men can still find themselves as victims who lack public empathy.

More than lacking empathy, they also lack the capacity to be seen as vulnerable. This is the core of institutional anti-Black misandry: people have difficulty perceiving Black male victimization because Black males are mythologized as "big game" (hypermasculine) to be hunted, and thus impervious to victimization in the eyes of white society and some Black feminists. This is most evident when Black men are aggressors and yet simultaneously victims; their vulnerability all but disappears. Black male celebrities such as Iceberg Slim, Ike Turner, Chris Brown, Bow Wow, and Richard Pryor were sexually victimized at a young age but are more remembered in the popular consciousness as uber-villains, abusers, and rapists—despite being lauded for being entertainers. In June 2011, Sugar Ray Leonard, beloved boxing phenom of the 1980s, publicly revealed for the first time in his autobiography *The Big Fight: My Life In And Out of the Ring* that:

> he was sexually abused as a young fighter by an unnamed prominent Olympic boxing coach. . . . He writes: "Before I knew it, he had unzipped

> my pants and put his hand, then mouth, on an area that has haunted me for life. I didn't scream. I didn't look at him. I just opened the door and ran."
> (Araton, 2011)

Aside from helping Black men create a vocabulary for their oppressive social experiences, *anti-Black misandry* also creates a method for conceptualizing issues with legal implications. For example, when addressing workplace sexual harassment and sexual discrimination, the primary model we have for that is women. In other words, women's experiences of being groped, orally disrespected, and denied hire or promotion on the basis of their sex have been well-documented. But how do Black males face racialized sexism in the workplace?

Racial-sexual discrimination against Black males presents differently than our traditional recollections of sexism as recalled by women. It often involves being mistreated in the workplace along lines that are reinforced by centuries-old racist stereotypes. In other words, for Black males, the most consistent stereotypes are those of violent, criminalistic, dangerous threats to everyone. To women, we are not only a violent threat, but a sexually violent threat, and thus the slightest suggestion that we have provided a sexual threat to someone (often levied without proof) is sufficient grounds for personal and professional ostracization or termination. If Black men are seen as threats, considered violent without cause, or described as "intimidating" or "scary," these are examples of anti-Black sexual discrimination. Instead of being groped or sexually propositioned as many women report, Black men often experience sexual discrimination on the basis of threat and have not been socialized to interpret such situations as discrimination. Thus, a man can be accused by co-workers who may not even be asked to produce a credible example, quote, physical gesture, etc. that illustrates how he was a threat. Rather, his threat is implicit because he exists. He may be fired outright without actual cause. In other words, the accusation is sufficient to justify guilt. This legacy goes back to the lynching of Black males for often imagined crimes without evidence (or trial). However, now it can be implemented with verbal, administrative, propagandistic, and/or career-related "violence." Yet this legacy has usually been one imposed by whites on Black folk, but now it can be imposed on gendered terms and never be regarded as such because gender is the sole purview of women and various LGBT demographics, and this need not be so. Yet what's important is why it happens: anti-Black misandry.

Black men need to argue for conceptual space using anti-Black misandry in gender discourses to challenge conventional gender narratives that ignore men, while unapologetically including Black male experiences as oppressed beings based on race and gender. More so, "males" and "men" are viewed as a homogenous grouping, even though males of color often have a contentious relationship with white masculinity, and much of the time Black males are more fervently attacked because of their gender rather than privileged by it.

Regarding legal protections, Black men should consider, when applicable, arguing for the special context of their oppression as "Black" + "men" using relevant legal policies. For example, with Title IX, one might consider:

> Section 1681. Sex (a) Prohibition against discrimination; exceptions. No person in the United States shall, on the basis of sex, be excluded from participation in, be denied the benefits of, or be subjected to discrimination under any education program or activity receiving Federal financial assistance.
>
> (Title IX Education Amendments, 1972)

And on gender harassment, Title IX continues:

> While it is clear that discrimination in violation of Title IX must be "on the basis of sex," courts have held that subjecting an individual to sex stereotyping may constitute sex discrimination in appropriate circumstances.
>
> (Title IX Legal Manual, "Gender Harassment")

Here, Title IX also applies to Black males who are being personally or institutionally discriminated against on the basis of sex and race, and Black males need to start using this information to alleviate themselves from racial and gendered threats. So in essence, people should know that the face of sex discrimination may not just be petite women enduring cat-calls in the workplace, but a 250 lb. dark-skinned Black male who may not smile very often.

To a certain degree, Black men, especially those seen publicly as hypermasculine (such as Sugar Ray Leonard) are not conceptualized as victims. Enter *anti-Black misandry*. This concept manifests in at least 13 key ways that merit definition and reflection. The first is *Anti-Black Misandric (ABM): Heterophobia*,

## *#1: ABM: Heterophobia*

According to Wake Forest University scholar of religion Ronald Neal, *ABM: Heterophobia* is the constructed idea that heterosexual Black men are to be hated because they are wicked, evil, and to be feared. In essence, heterophobia is the fear of straight Black men. This has a long history stemming from the chattel slave era and is the impetus behind the many rape accusations, lynchings, instances of police brutality, town massacres, and high incarceration rates faced by Black men. With *ABM: Heterophobia*, white women can sexually dominate Black men while accusing Black men of being aggressors, using the law (and public perception of Black men) much the same way lynch mobs were used during slavery to coerce men into their sexual service. Meanwhile, heterosexual Black men are often sought after by white men as "big game," or in other words, those with martial authority (or vigilantes) who hunt Black men for sport. This is the cause of many police killings of unarmed Black men, men seen as both a threat and the means for demonstrating social dominance.

Ironically, *ABM: Heterophobia* can be seen in research from the most popular theoreticians on Black masculinity: bell hooks. In her assessment of the *Central Park 5*, a group of young Black men accused of having raped a white woman in Central Park in New York. She stated,

> No one can truly believe that the young black males involved in the Central Park incident were not engaged in a suicidal ritual enactment of a dangerous masculinity that will ultimately threaten their lives, their well-being. If one reads again Michael Dyson's piece "The Plight of Black Men," focusing especially on the part where he describes the reason many young black men form gangs—"the sense of absolute belonging and unsurpassed love"—it is easy to understand why young black males are despairing and nihilistic. And it is rather naive to think that if they do not value their own lives, they will value the lives of others. Is it really so difficult for folks to see the connection between the constant pornographic glorification of male violence against women that is represented, enacted, and condoned daily in the culture and the Central Park crime?
>
> (hooks, 1999)

In *We Real Cool* (2004), hooks further frames Black male sexuality—and its assumed penchant for "fucking" (i.e., patriarchal hypersexuality)—as an extension of white male sexual norms mimetically appropriated by Black men.

> Those Black males who wanted to let the world know that they were engaged in the patriarchal sex that centralized fucking could do so by spreading their seed and making babies. In segregated Black communities men in power (political leaders, the clergy, teachers) used their authority to sexually harass or seduce willing and unwilling females. Equating manhood with fucking, many Black men saw status and economic success as synonymous with endless sexual conquest.
>
> (hooks, 2004)

This type of pathological villainization of hetero-Black male sexuality has been heavily influenced by white racist scholarship, a point philosopher and Black Male Studies scholar Tommy J. Curry explains well when he states:

> In order to sustain the mythical analysis of Black men as violent sexual predators, gender theory often depends on racist sociological and criminological theories developed in late 1960s and 1970s. Subculture of violence theory was the most popular of these theories and grew out of the racist "ghetto-culture" literature from the 1930s–1960s.

> In 2004, bell hooks published what is now the most cited book on Black masculinity using these theories to explain Black male homicide, domestic abuse, and rape. Black Male Studies has a decolonial motivation and continues to demonstrate how gender theories' account of Black masculinity depends on pathological models of white social science to explain Black male deviance and socialization.
>
> Black scholars will continue to ignore this clear connection between subculture and contra-culture of violence theory and contemporary Black masculinity theory. It is exactly the same. Almost verbatim. The acceptance of gender theory and intersectionality is partially rooted in its extension of racist logic.
>
> The reality is that in the 21st century Black Studies endorses the very same racist theories it sought to refute in the 1970s because we now call it feminist or intersectional. Racism and anti-Black misandry is now normalized throughout disciplines and scholarship.
>
> (Curry, 2020)

*ABM Heterophobia* is critical of the fear and mischaracterization of Black male sexuality with subculture and contra-culture of violence theory, and thus also with hooks' theories regarding Black males. Regarding subculture of violence theory, Curry states,

> Menachem Amir's *Patterns in Forcible Rape* introduced a *subculture of violence theory* claiming to explain why poor Black men became accustomed to committing rape and how Black women as mothers and partners contributed to the transmission of these values from childhood to adulthood.
>
> Amir introduced the most prominent cultural explanation of Black male sexual aggression in the 20th century. Whereas previous ethnological formulations of the Black male rapist relied on ontogenic accounts of racial development, Amir introduced a theory that focused on the deviant values of Negroes and how these racial norms within the Black race produced Black male rapists. He writes:
>
> The Negro subculture is an historically unique subculture which embodies all the characteristics of a lower-class subculture but has some of its features in a more pronounced form. . . . The Negro subculture is characterized by the revolving of life around some basic focal concerns which include a search for thrills through aggressive actions and sexual exploits. . . . The emphasis is given by males to masculinity, and their need to display and defend it through brief and transitory relations with women. Such needs and the subsequent concerns with sex stems from growing up in a family in which the mother is dominant and the father has a marginal position. . . . Young boys are imbued with negative, or at least ambivalent, feelings toward masculine functions. Sexual and aggressive behavior becomes

> the main vehicle for asserting their worthiness. They, therefore, idealize personal violence and prowess which substitute for social and economic advantages.
>
> (Curry, 2021)

The appropriation of subculture of violence theory into Black feminism and Africana Studies has made elements of the field heterophobic in a distinctly misandric fashion, and with hooks as the face of it, it is often not critiqued for fear of being labeled misogynistic, a deflective gesture that Amir's theories would not have received were his ideas introduced to Africana Studies directly.

Interestingly, *anti-Black misandric heterophobia* can also be experienced by Black women. Tatyana Hargrove of Bakersfield, CA, was "confronted by police at gunpoint, punched in the mouth and bitten by a police dog after being mistaken for a much larger bald man suspected of threatening people with a machete" in July 2017. The *Atlanta Black Star* states that:

> Hargrove, who was wearing a hat, "appeared to be a male and matched the description of the suspect that had brandished the machete and was also within the same complex the suspect had fled to," the arresting officer, Christopher Moore, wrote in a report obtained by the Californian. He thought she had a weapon in her bag. Moore said he didn't realize Hargrove was female until she told him her first name.
>
> "I'm a girl. I just don't dress like one," she said. The suspected machete-wielder, Douglas Washington, 24, was arrested the next day and remained jailed.
>
> (Associated Press, 2017)

Misandry functions across gender and sexuality in that even Black gay males face it for at least two reasons: 1) often, most do not know which Black men are gay, and 2) they are still Black men. For Black females, heterophobia can stem from the stereotypical legacy of Black female masculinization. This tradition saw Black women as masculine, thus marking them as "not-women."

### *#2: ABM: Male Feminization*

The second version of *anti-Black misandry* is *ABM: Male Feminization* in which the fear of Black men's sexuality in society is rooted in a seemingly contradictory conceptualization of Black manhood by white society as a dysfunctional male (feminine; inferior) counterpart to white masculine sexual norms. Thus, regardless of sexuality, Black men were considered: effeminate, dependent, hypersexual, and sexually violent. This is the legacy of 19th- and 20th-century ethnologists and their inhumane worldview of Black men. Historically, they have considered Black men to be effeminate in the sense that they are considered emasculated and feminine in contrast to Western masculinity. Black males are considered dependent because they are child-like, weak, unintelligent, and incapable. They are considered hypersexual in the sense that they are seen as hypermasculine and sexually deviant by 20th-century ethnologists especially, and lastly that they are sexually violent, especially post-slavery, a notion used to justify lynchings and hyper-incarceration.

The reason for the *effeminate*, *dependent*, *hypersexual*, and *sexually violent* labels is that as threatening, virile, and potent as Black manhood is, the denigration of it by white men only seems to affirm their own superiority. By metaphorically, proverbially, sexually, and institutionally "effeminizing" Black manhood and labeling it as defective somehow, white manhood remains the standard for its ideal configuration. This is why this assault on Black manhood via its definitional sexual composition applies to Black men regardless of their sexuality. Straight, gay, bi, and trans Black men were raped by empowered white men without repercussion to enforce white sexual dominance. And this assault is initiated on terms divorced from what Black manhood actually is and only concerns itself with what it defines Black manhood as.

It should be noted that regardless of whether it is a matter of anti-Black homo- or heterophobia, Black men who are lynched often experience sexualized threats. They can be penetrated, castrated, sodomized, or otherwise violated in terms of their genitalia. Such was the case for Théo, a 22-year-old French youth worker, who was anally raped by a police officer in France in 2017 (Holley, 2017). Or Darrin Manning, a 16-year-old student in Philadelphia whose testicles were ruptured (squeezed by hand until crushed) by a white female police officer in 2014 (Murdock, 2014). There are many historical lynchings where Black men's genitalia have been removed and grotesquely put on display afterward.

Intra-racially, Black male feminization is the hallmark of Black queerness in popular consciousness, as lesbianism is slightly more acceptable in Western culture mainly because of its eroticism for many men. The reasons that spur mainstream fascination with Black male effeminateness in Black contexts range. Some believe that Black gay males disrupt families because they do not often contribute to the continuing bloodline of a given family (this may also explain why lesbianism is not as denigrated). Yet the primary reason for intra-racial, anti-Black male femophobia is the internalization of negative sexual values extended by white society. In other words, Black sexuality was hyper-eroticized during and after slavery, and Black people were seen as sexually deviant in contrast to normative white sexuality. This initiated a sort of sexual hyper-conservatism after slavery (as embodied by the Black Church) and led to a sound denunciation of all things deemed sexually deviant that may seem to reinforce stereotypes about Black sexual exoticism. Such stereotypes served to help rationalize the abusive sexualization and prostitution of Black bodies that still exist to this day. Yet few acknowledge that this exoticism had more to do with Western white projections of deviance to establish its normative status than anything Black men were actually doing.

### *#3: ABM: Phallophobia*

The third version of anti-Black misandry is *ABM: Phallophobia*, the fear of the Black male phallus, not only resulting in a fear of straight Black men but all biologically born Black and male. This also refers to Black male-to-female trans-women based on the idea that if born Black and male, one remains a sexual threat to women. For Black female-to-male trans-men, they are perceived as a threat because they appear as biological Black men and thus are perennially violent rapists. For example, Nigerian feminist Chimamanda Ngozi Adichie offended transgender women when she stated in a 2017 interview,

> I think if you've lived in the world as a man with the privileges that the world accords to men and then sort of change gender, it's difficult for me to accept that then we can equate your experience with the experience of a woman who has lived from the beginning as a woman and who has not been accorded those privileges that men are.
>
> ("Chimamanda Ngozi Adichie Sparks Debate About Privilege With Comments On Trans Women," 2017)

Her comments were not focused on trans-men, but only trans-women. Nevertheless, she underscored many cis-gender Black women's feelings, suggesting that only "former males" could not truly be another gender, but not trans-men (formerly biologically females). Additionally, she did not suggest that post-op trans-men now had privilege. In such a manner, any born Black and female can avoid any type of privilege (or critique), but Black males—regardless of sexual orientation—are subject to the permanent status of being patriarchs who covet privilege.

Similarly, despite much of the gender-neutral language used to address transgender access laws, most that opposed them in 2016–2017 seemed to do so out of fear of trans-women . . . again, former males. As stated, in a Time.com article, "Allowing transgender people to use the restroom that aligns with their gender identity will end up letting male sexual predators into women's bathrooms" (Steinmetz, 2016). Although this statement does not reference any exact statistics, it is interesting to note how female predators have become non-existent in this dynamic, and this is exacerbated in sports. Comedian and fight announcer Joe Rogan and online personality Bas Rutten came out in strong opposition to Mixed Martial Arts (MMA) fighter Fallon Fox receiving licensing with Rogan stating,

> First of all, she's not really a "she." She's a transgender, post-op person. The operation doesn't shave down your bone density. It doesn't change. You look at a man's hands and you look at a woman's hands and they're built different. They're just thicker, they're stronger, your wrists are thicker, your elbows are thicker, your joints are thicker. Just the mechanical

function of punching, a man can do it much harder than a woman can, period.

(Noble, 2017)

Along similar lines, transgender Olympic athlete Semenya Caster of South Africa was critiqued for winning the women's 800m in 2016 at the Olympics in Brazil (Longman, 2016). The contrast, however, may be racial. Famous Olympic athlete Bruce Jenner became "Caitlyn" to worldwide fanfare and attention, while Chris Mosier became the lauded, first trans-male athlete to join an official Olympics team. In 2013, Mosier was named Athlete of the Year at LA's Compete Sports Diversity Awards ("New Sports Ad Stars First Transgender Olympian," 2016). Here, both a trans-woman and a trans-man received praise for their efforts, while Black trans-athletes were met with skepticism and doubt, alongside narratives of manipulation and exploitation.

### *#4: ABM: Disposability*

The fourth version of *anti-Black misandry* is *ABM: Disposability*, a concept that refers to widely ignored Black male struggles, difficulties, and victimization. Much of this text refers to African American males and contexts, but evidence of this concept can be found when addressing the kidnapping of 276 Nigerian girls by the terrorist group Boko Haram in 2014. Although the focus is not really on their kidnapping but on the American fascination with it, the event became a focal point for an international feminist sensibility, spawning the Twitter hashtag *#BringBackOurGirls*. Yet the burning alive of 59 Nigerian boys by Boko Haram a few months prior went virtually ignored (Rothman, 2014). So did the subsequent killings of boys and men in mid-August of 2014, where men's rights activists on *www.AVoiceforWomen.com* reported that "Boko Haram organized another raid in the northeastern part of Nigeria, this time kidnapping 97 men and boys and killing 28 other men. Additionally, 6 older men were killed as the raid ended, raising the total death toll to 34." The article goes further to suggest that, "It appears that the Western world can think of the Nigerian girls as 'our girls' but is unable to think of the brutally massacred boys as 'our boys'" (Vâlsan, 2014). *Anti-Black male disposability* suggests that this is so, as its principle argument is that males' experiences, even when tragic, can quickly become background "white noise" to what is normatively considered daily life.

In a seemingly more subtle context, young Black males are socially prepared for disposability at an early age. Usually, through toys and sports, they are socialized to revere male heroism and seek public approval, an idea that proposes they selflessly sacrifice themselves for others to attain social approval. Sports are similar—and interestingly, the focus of many young Black male career goals. In sports such as football and basketball, two of the most highly patronized sports for young Black males, both emphasize team play and sacrifice for the group. Still, this type of disposability can be abusive, where some families exploit their son's abilities for status and wealth (men's rights activist Warren Ferrell considers this a unique form of misandrist child abuse). For example, NFL athlete Tyron Smith had to file a restraining order against his own family because they demanded more despite what he gifted them upon gaining his professional contract. As such,

> Smith, the first offensive lineman selected in 2011 when the Cowboys drafted him ninth overall out of USC, signed a four-year, $12.5 million contract. He gave his family a substantial amount of money, agreeing to pay his parents in four installments. But Smith's stepfather, Roy Pinkney, his mother, Frankie Pinkney, and some of his siblings kept coming back for more.
>
> "There was a certain amount I agreed to give them, but it went way beyond that, and I was just like, 'I'm done,'" Smith said. "I feel like I shouldn't have given them so much. There was nothing wrong with helping them out and making sure they were taken care of, but not something to where they live the same lifestyle as you."
>
> ("6 Stunning Details We Learned In Cowboys' Tyron Smith Family Saga," 2013)

Nevertheless, the training many Black boys get in disposability is early preparation for adult disposability. Although a bevy of the jobs available to Black males are life-threatening, many of them have spent most of their adolescence learning about sacrifice. So as police officers, firemen, truck drivers, janitors, prisoners, garbage men, soldiers, and even gang members are subject to life-threatening conditions to earn an income, their deaths are often not acknowledged. In fact, private transportation service workers suffered the most in 2015, according to the Bureau of Labor Statistics. Most total deaths (1,264) were due to roadway accidents among private company truck drivers (Census of Fatal Occupational Injuries, 2015). As service workers—the majority male—such jobs denote a disposable quality, and Black men find themselves in such professions in high numbers. Still, the disproportionate number of Black male convicts is probably the most overt example of Black male disposability, especially when coupled with the judicial system's disregard for Black male life regarding sentencing.

For example, Pennsylvania native Joseph Ligon was "convicted for the 1953 murders of two people at the age of 15, [but] has maintained his innocence for more than half a century" (Zilber, 2016). He has been in prison for 63 years and at 79 years old is "the longest-serving juvenile lifer in the world." After a recent U.S. Supreme Court decision deemed mandatory life sentences for juvenile offenders unconstitutional, Ligon declined on principle, arguing that he wouldn't accept parole but rather wanted his innocence acknowledged. Scores of Black men have likely found themselves incarcerated for lengths of time that are disproportionately longer than other demographics. Ligon's experience is a clear demonstration of *anti-Black male disposability*.

Another type of disposability is the obliviousness to Black male infants' treatment by industries such as the school system, the prison industrial complex, and the school-to-prison pipeline, as well as their treatment by family and caregivers. For instance, India Kirksey, an Ohio woman, raped her 4-year-old son and posted the video on the Periscope live-streaming app for others to see (Sommerfeldt, 2017). Another, Brooklyn caretaker, Zarah Coombs, "beat her 4-year-old son Zamair to death with a broomstick after the preschooler accidentally broke an egg on the floor of their Brooklyn basement apartment, sources said" (Mai et al., 2017). In another case, a 19-year-old Michigan mother named Jazmine Nichole Pacyga performed fellatio on her own 3-month-old son for money (upon arrest, she received a $200,000 bail, while the white man who asked for the porn photos received a $500,000 bail) (Miller, 2017). Lastly, another young mother killed her 3-month-old son for crying too much by smothering him in a blanket and striking him until he fell silent. Hours later, she took his slain body, along with her 3-year-old daughter, shopping with her—avoiding having to tell the child's father that his son was dead (Thompson, 2011). Interestingly, none of these reports got any major news coverage yet each directly impacted Black males.

According to the *Child Trends Databank* and the *Centers for Disease Control*,

> Infants are most likely to be killed by their mother during the first week of life, but thereafter are more likely to be killed by a male (usually their father or stepfather). . . . The infant homicide rate increased from 4.3 per 100,000 in 1970, to 9.2 in 2000, before declining to 7.2 per 100,000 in 2013. . . . In most years, males have been more likely than females to be killed during the first year of life. In 2013, for example, the infant homicide rate for boys was 8.7 per 100,000 children under age one, and 5.5 for girls. This gap has generally widened since 1970.
>
> (Overpeck et al., 1998)

So, even though the data shows that Black male infants are more susceptible to infanticide by both mothers and fathers, along with the mistreatment of even infant Black males—whether focusing on child maltreatment, abuse, sexual assault, rape, or murder—few seem to publicly acknowledge that Black males experience these issues in any serious manner deserving of acknowledgment.

### *#5: ABM: Appropriation*

The fifth version of *anti-Black misandry* is *ABM: Appropriation*: when groups appropriate Black male life issues and experiences when convenient for their agendas but "bait and switch" them for others' agendas once an adequate amount of attention has been achieved. Here, political organizations, artists, and entertainers often appropriate Black male aesthetics and experiences while disregarding Black male life. Performers such as Elvis Presley or Vanilla Ice have historically been known for absorbing Black male musical aesthetics and personas while never acknowledging the plight of Black males (even the plight of Black male performers exploited by the same recording industry these white artists are awarded by).

### *#6: ABM: Homoeroticism*

The sixth version of *anti-Black misandry* is *ABM: Homoeroticism.* As characterized by Tommy J. Curry in his description of Vincent Woodard's text, *The Delectable Negro, anti-Black male cannibalistic homoeroticism* is "the literal and figurative consumption of the Black male body—the eating of the Black male (cannibalism) sustained by the homoerotic sexual urge of racism" (Curry, 2017). Such cannibalism need not be literal—although historically it most assuredly has been—but can be symbolic in that society absorbs Black male bodies and labor without regard to their health. The eroticism found in white men's domination of Black men is by virtue sexualized and suggests a transfer of sexual power, as "hypermasculine" Black men are seen as conquests by white men, as "big game" to be hunted and dominated to claim their hypermasculinity. This can happen via sex or violence.

Some white couples participate in anti-Black male homoeroticism by exploiting Black men's sexual labor for fetishistic purposes. On amateur pornographic websites (referring to everyday people, not porn actors) and in private society, white couples entertain cuckolding relationships with Black men. In these dynamics, white men pay Black men to have sex with their wives or themselves while their wives seemingly revel in Black men's phallic and sexual performance. In some videos, these white men even perform cunnilingus on their women after sexual intercourse has ended, consuming the remains in the name of sexual exoticism (where Black men's semen is symbolic of masculine virility, sheepishly consumed in grotesque fashion as a testament to white male inferiority). Despite the apparent power dynamics of Black males performatively "raping" white women and dominating white men by having them watch helplessly, it is quite the reverse beneath the surface. White men control the dynamic off-camera, as they often pay these Black male studs while giving their wives permission to have such exotic sex. In other words, they control all facets of the engagement and only appear exploited because they wish it so, meaning it fits their sexual fetish. Still, these Black men are sexually exploited (often for money), objectified, "consumed" (literally in terms of the example here, or figuratively when regarding that once "used" for their sexual utility, they are discarded haphazardly) and used for white sexual fantasies stemming from stereotypes of Black men.

Regarding violence and homoerotic cannibalism, one example occurred in March 2017. "A white U.S. army veteran killed a man in New York after traveling there specifically to kill Black people, according to police. James Harris Jackson chose a man at random and killed him with a sword, according to police (Silva, 2017). The attack was intended as 'an assault' on the city's inclusiveness and diversity, authorities said. The man from Baltimore turned himself in at a Times Square police station, about 25 hours after he had killed Timothy Caughman, who had staggered into a precinct bleeding to death" (Griffin, 2017).

> Jackson wandered the streets in a long black coat, carrying a 26-inch sword. He then encountered Mr. Caughman, who was collecting bottles from rubbish bins, according to police. He was stabbed repeatedly in the chest and back, apparently at random. Mr. Caughman was 66 years old and lived nearby. He was taken to hospital by police after he arrived at the station, and later died in hospital from his wounds.
>
> (Griffin, 2017)

Another example of *ABM: Homoeroticism* dynamic is convict Darren Rainey (Ferner, 2017). A convict serving time at the Dade Correctional Institution in South Florida, official reports suggest no wrongdoing, arguing that Rainey's death was an accident. However, an independent investigation suggests that four guards likely subjected Rainey to water temperatures exceeding 180 degrees by some reports for two hours (Geiling, 2017), as third-degree burns are produced at 150 degrees. Some prisoners said they heard Rainey screaming that the water was too hot and that he could not take it anymore before he was "found dead lying face up in the shower, his skin red and slipping off" (Safdar, 2017).

A whistleblower in the case, an orderly in the mental health ward and a fellow inmate named Harold Hempstead serving a 160+ year sentence for burglary kept a detailed diary of inmate abuse and was relocated to another prison (assumed as a measure to silence him from publicizing his assertions that prison guards punished prisoners using scalding hot showers as a torture method). He asserts, "Rainey, who suffered from mental illness, had been forced into a specially rigged shower by corrections officers who had been using scalding showers to punish inmates for bad behavior" (Brown, 2017). Strangely enough, the state attorney deferred to Dr. Emma Lew, the medical examiner who ruled that the cause of death was not from any burns—in fact arguing that he had no burns. She ruled that the cause of death was "schizophrenia, heart disease and 'confinement to a shower.'" It would seem Rainey was tortured to death as punishment within the prison (Brown, 2017).

The deeply embedded hatred of Black men in our society (anti-Black misandry), is not just about not being able to get a job or being called a nigger, etc. Although those are examples of hatred, Jackson's actions are what the specific hatred of Black men looks like. He is only one person of many whose "work" killing Black men has been discovered. Others have accumulated their own killings of Black men, even creating their own "mass graves," collections of Black male victims that feed them a sense of dominant virility upon their victimization. Such can range from:

- judges or attorney prosecutors who habitually participate in sending scores of Black men to prisons or death row with little to no evidence,
- cops who kill Black men and are never punished for it,
- blue-collar managers to firemen/police captains who routinely give Black men the most dangerous types of work assignments while reserving the easiest and safest for white employees,
- feminists who affirm white stereotypes of Black male hypermasculinity and advocate for punitive state-imposed solutions against Black men that include incarceration and death using de-contextualized events and narratives while avoiding large-scale data,
- teachers who routinely condemn Black boys to special education because they don't want to deal with them, ignoring the "track" this can place them on that routes them out of educational opportunity and into prisons and death,
- women who falsely accuse them of arrestable crimes they didn't commit out of revenge or demonstrations of power, or
- politicians and judges who create policies regarding redlining in neighborhoods or impose arrest policies to increase the number of private/state/federal-run prisons that disproportionately warehouse and kill Black men for political profit and kickbacks—and are rarely punished for it.

Anti-Black male homoerotic cannibalism is real. It is not some vague declaration of hate that somehow is supposed to exist yet only "oppresses" a group by framing nebulous micro-aggressions that make one feel bad about something arbitrary, but this is not the case. This is a matter of life and death. It is ignored, and it has been going on for generations. The report that came out recently said 1.5 million Black men were missing. Yet, whites and Black feminists ignored it because it was irrelevant to them, including issues like the tradition of hunters who collect and kill Black men for sport and only occasionally get revealed (Wolfers et al., 2015). They may not all have white hoods and actual mass graves in their backyards. Some merely have a list of names of Black men to whose deaths they contributed and will never have to answer for their crimes.

### *#7: ABM: Homophilia/Transphilia*

The seventh version is *ABM: Homophilia/Transphilia*. The Black male image is represented as a sort of fetishistic homophilia or transphilia in media. When this occurs, it is: 1) highly stereotypical, exaggerated, stereotypically flamboyant (code for gay) fashion, or 2) as "masculine" women. Such stereotypes promote the faulty idea that Black gay men are not men subject to racist assault, racism, etc. The fetishizing of Black male homosexuality marks Black gay men as effeminate.

In the Black sketch comedy show *In Living Color* (1990–1994), comedians Damon Wayans' and David Alan Grier play gay characters Blaine Edwards and Antoine Merriweather (respectively), stereotypically gay Black men who opine on media. Overly effeminate, hypersexual, and ambiguously gay or trans, such representations cast Black gay men as comedic and fetishistically inane. A fixture in Hollywood culture, ideas about masculine Black male characters being represented as effeminate (in drag) shows Black men (especially hypermasculine men) in bad drag. Representations of "masculine" women accomplish at least three goals: 1) to effeminize Black men and secure them in the American (and global) imagination as "not-men," 2) to make them laughably grotesque, and 3) to signify Black women to suggest that they, too, are "not-women." This *anti-Black male homophilia* fetishizes popular media's conception of Black and gay as something curious and yet somehow laughably effeminate about all Black males. This confirms not only longstanding myths about Black men as less than masculine by Western standards but also separates Black heterosexual men from homosexual men in the popular imagination, presenting them as less "manly" despite the fact that they are subject to the same ills that most Black men face daily.

Homophilia is an important feature of misandry in that when studying or analyzing homosexuality, there is often a strong emphasis on the femininity of male homosexuality. It is considered the only redeeming factor about gay men, not because they are gay but because they are men. The femininity of male homosexuality is thus lauded as worthy of analysis and considered a revolutionary method for re-conceptualizing masculinity. However, the masculinity of Black homosexual men—the masculinity that still marks gay Black men as "male" in the public sphere—is wholly disregarded. This also cements their non-masculinity/femininity for most. Regardless of sexuality, Black men are considered threats for simply being, and Black gay men are not excused from such perceptions. Hence, the misandry Black gay males experience—even in the academy—is rooted in the fetishization of their femininity and the hatred (and imposed invisibility) of their masculinity.

### *#8: ABM: Sexual Objectification*

The eighth version is *ABM: Sexual Objectification*, a term that refers to Black men who are sexually objectified in at least two ways: 1) by being expected to serve the sexual gratification of others strictly, or 2) to serve as "success objects" for others' financial gratification. Black men are assumed to "always want sex" and are therefore assumed to only function as walking phalluses to be enjoyed by others at their behest. They are also expected to serve as "success objects" that provide others with financial support. In essence, as a colleague once said, "too many women feel like a man is their retirement plan, even when they make more money than you" (Anonymous, phone conversation, July 1, 2017). This may take the form of supplementing a person's lifestyle, paying child support after having been manipulated into impregnating someone who intended on using them for resources mitigated through family court, raising others' children, divorcing someone who uses their court-awarded alimony indefinitely, or performing stereotypically gendered tasks (such as repair or pay for household repairs, provide protection from violence, etc.). In essence, Black men are sexually objectified in regard to their class/career status, marriageability, financial resources, assertiveness (read as "manly"), virility, penises size/length, and sexual prowess.

A common yet under-reported phenomenon is the objectification of Black male athletes as successful objects to families and intimate partners. For example, Phillip Buchanon, former NFL athlete and author of *New Money: Staying Rich* (Buchanon, 2015), who describes how his mother demanded $1 million dollars for raising him (Dubin, 2016). Such is an example of using Black men as 'success objects.'

Another example of this phenomenon would be that of a "Brooklyn woman . . . [who hired a hit man and] was sentenced to life in prison without the possibility of parole for killing her husband—for $900,000 in insurance money that would clear up her debt" (Carrega, 2017). Wife Alishia Noel-Murray decided to kill her husband for insurance money and hired Kirk Portious for $3,500 to do the deed. The strange part is that even when men (assassins) get caught being proxies for women's violence, few women are held accountable for the crimes, so Noel-Murray is a bit of an anomaly in that she was even arrested.

On a similar note, 45-year-old Uloma Curry-Walker,

> could receive life in prison without parole for the November 2013 slaying of William Walker, whom she had married just four months earlier. Prosecutors said Curry-Walker was nearing financial ruin after running up tens of thousands of dollars in debt when she asked her then-17-year-old daughter and the daughter's boyfriend to find someone to kill her husband so she could collect the insurance money.
>
> (The Associated Press, 2017)

Warren Ferrell points out that when male spouses kill their wives, they usually kill themselves as well. On the other hand, female spouses often kill for money (e.g., life insurance or wealth inheritance). He argues that poorer women use sex to initiate other men to kill, while wealthier women use the money to pay other men to kill their husbands. This, in turn, leads some to suggest that men are the only ones who kill their spouses, and again re-affirms female innocence (Ferrell, 1994). But proxy violence often goes undetected and is seldom recorded when calculations are made regarding women's violence. Still, in the final equation, Noel-Murray killed for money, meaning that her husband became a "financial object" to her. Hence, she objectified him on financial grounds, exemplifying anti-Black male sexual objectification.

### *#9: ABM: Social Incompetence*

The ninth form of *anti-Black misandry* is *ABM: Social Incompetence*. Black men are often seen as failed patriarchs or incompetent beings. They are considered almost childlike beings who have to be managed by either dominant white men or "strong" Black women. From sitcoms to lived experiences, expectations of Black male failure have a deep-seated history in American culture and intra-racially in the African American community. Tropes regarding failure stem back to Black men "failing" to sufficiently resist European slavers to "failing" to destroy the very institution of slavery in America. The failure is reinvented almost generationally when Black men suffer from unemployment, heightened incarceration, police-sanctioned murder, and a variety of other issues that prevent them from playing ideal familial roles.

### *#10: ABM: Transference*

The tenth form of *anti-Black misandry* is *Transference*. For African American males, the behavior of one is used to reflect on the entire racial group in media, securing the notion that Black males are inherently inferior, cowardly, abusive, criminalistic, and are the antithesis of masculinity. In contrast, a single white male's accomplishments are often used to reflect on all white men, securing the notion that white men are inherently superior and are the standard for masculinity. *ABM: Transference* addresses this bifurcated dynamic by suggesting that the denigration of Black males is purposeful and used to socially engineer a negative public perception of Black males to ensure their social exclusion. In other words, stereotypes regarding Black males can be consistently reinforced by hyper-focusing on individuals who seem to affirm them, while reinforcing white superiority by hyper-focusing on accomplished white males who exhibit competence and success.

### *#11: Course and Refined ABM*

The eleventh form is "Course" and "Refined" anti-Black misandry. *Course ABM* refers to the blatant dehumanization evident on social media. Much of it centers around criminalizing Black men on carceral issues. It is often crass, offensive, and brazenly misandric. An example of such might be when Black men are referred to as "bullet bags" who should die because they are less capable than white men (a term that trended on Twitter in 2021. The other term is *Refined ABM* and is more reserved. It deceptively appears objective, especially when espoused by professional feminist judges, academics, politicians, or therapists. Often, their arguments stem from *subculture of violence theory*, an intellectual justification for anti-Black misandry rooted in racist white ethnology (Curry, 2021). It can purposefully be targeted to harm or be passive-aggressively dismissive.

An example of *Refined ABM* might be a Twitter post on January 12, 2022 by Dr. Kristen E. Broady, Policy Director of The Hamilton Project and a Fellow of Economic Studies at The Brookings Institution. She stated, "The growing racial disparity in employment underscores that the economic recovery is still being impeded by systemic bias against Black workers—particularly, Black women and Black teens." With this quote, she posted a chart entitled, "Table 2. U.S. unemployment rate by race, gender, and age, December 2020 to December 2021," from Brookings Metro, sourced from the U.S. Bureau of Labor Statistics (2022). When challenged on Twitter she defended her comments by pointing out that Black teens had the highest unemployment rates (at one point up to 24%). She then stated that what she said about Black women was "accurate." Yet the point of contention by those who wrote in the thread was that she purposefully avoided addressing Black men when making her observations about the chart. Teens constituted both Black young men and women, and many suspected that based on the presented data it was likely Black males who increased the teens' numbers. She ignored that as a single demographic, Black males held the highest unemployment (up to 10.5%), exceeding even Black women (up to 8.9%), whom she took the time to comment on specifically. She is a professional researcher, and her comments represent Refined ABM in that she casually avoided acknowledging the single demographic most adversely affected, suggesting that were she able to influence policy (which such data is produced to help influence), her willingness to determine whom we should focus on is skewed and somewhat oblivious to Black males specifically.

### *#12: Familial Demotion/Discharge*

The twelfth form is *ABM: Familial Demotion/Discharge*. It argues that feminist gender theory, mainstream media, and women's casual culture downplay Black males' relevance to families and have repelled many Black men. Thus, in response, Black men have avoided traditional family participation since the 1960s. Use of condoms during sex, ritual non-monogamy, life strategies emphasizing non-marital practices to avoiding dating/mating with single mothers, long-term sexual abstinence, parental abandonment, and their overall support for informal relationship practices all might represent an unwillingness to participate in environments that are socially hostile to Black males. And this is despite Black fathers still spending more time with their children and paying child support more than any other group of men, according to Judge Joe Brown (WeAllBeTV, 2015). Such has been made worse because Black women have been enabled to use law enforcement institutions to control or discipline Black men on a whim.

### *#13: ABM: Gentrification*

The thirteenth and final form is *ABM: Gentrification*. This focuses on the gentrification of Black life in policy, law enforcement, media, entrepreneurship, employment, education, and the family itself. The process of this unique form of gentrification reconstructs Black women as a new buffer class. This gentrification is enforced by an outside group in a manner that dramatically influences the cultural and material institutions of another group's community on racial, class, and gendered grounds. Much like buying up the real estate of another community and deciding who can occupy it, white society defines our worth by access to resources we do not control. In seven key areas, Black men find themselves without support.

In terms of gender rights, there is a palpable absence of legal rights targeted at Black men. The language of Title IX is disingenuously written in a gender-neutral fashion, but its application's spirit is misandric to Black men. "Gender" only truly references women. In terms of reproduction, there is a critical absence of biological rights for Black men in that there is no comparable range of birth control options as there are for women. Regarding law enforcement, there is an absence of justice from the War on Drugs to the Three Strikes Law to police homicide in general. Media entertainment is corporate-owned and often female-focused, as female consumers are those responsive to media and consume the most. The result is often media that targets their interests to the expense of men and boys by creating a dearth of representations of strong heterosexual Black male archetypes while asserting female-superiority tropes. In terms of employment and entrepreneurship, Black women have leveraged double-minority status and maintained more consistent employment for decades, while young Black men, for example, in 35 major cities are 40–50% unemployed. Unheard-of numbers in any community! Regarding economic resources for entrepreneurship, the pandemic evidenced that there were no significant resources for Black men, despite them having more businesses than Black women (and both often start businesses with no capital). Yet a series of companies targeted Black women for advancement such as Goldman Sachs (who promised $10 billion dollars), VISA, Mastercard, and others. Beyond the pandemic there remains a critical absence of substantive Black male-targeted economic and infrastructural support. Anything else is aspirational but lacks substantive support that other demographics have enjoyed for generations. In terms of education, state-financed support for women (especially Pell Grants ex-con males cannot have) helps them to attain more college degrees than Black men, helping to constitute a grave absence of quality education due to unparalleled levels of expulsion, detention, racial and gendered low-grading, relegations to special education, lack of curriculum targeting young Black males, and limited college track courses. Lastly, the Black family's access to state support (e.g., welfare, housing, food, daycare, and family court) contributed to the absence of Black men by requiring their absence for the family to receive it.

Altogether, these seven areas alone helped to produce a new buffer class of educated, employed Black women while underdeveloping Black males across ages. *ABM: Gentrification*, then, refers to a process of gentrification that is leveraged institutionally and by policy.

# 4 Flat Blackness, Flat Maleness, and Black Andromortality

## I. Flat Blackness

The conceptual idea of flattening simply refers to a collapsing of nuance. This chapter will talk about the flattening of nuance regarding notions of blackness and maleness. Contrary to popular approaches to gender analysis, women, girls, and LGBTs seem to be the priority focus. But this text presupposes that there is more to discuss about males, particularly Black males, than conventionally thought. Most of the time it is generically assumed that we know all we need to know about heterosexual males simply because they seem to of been the focus of generations' worth of research. But part of Black Male Studies' focus is that we still have not learned to study Black males outside the framework of stereotype, conjecture, and pathology. That said, *flatness*, as it pertains to race and gender, has been used in a manner that alienated and underdeveloped public reflections of Black manhood.

Conceptually, flatness pertains to race, gender, and more, particularly regarding men. It most often occurs by abstraction, meaning it is not what is said about blackness or maleness, it's what is not said. It is the absence of openly and purposely regarding Black males that is at issue. For example, in 2021, Xfinity launched a pro-Black woman Olympics commercial between Black History Month and Women's History Month (Johnson, 2021). The theme of the commercial was breaking boundaries, and it highlighted Black women who were breaking expectations and boundaries set against women. At a certain point, they pointed out that a particular "Black sprinter" broke boundaries, and then two "Black women" followed suit. This was supposed to be motivational and inspirational, but instead it was insulting. And as much as they wanted to focus on the upliftment of women, the way they chose to do so was to downplay that sprinter named Jesse Owens. If one did not know who Jesse Owens was, one would not think much of it. But because of the celebrity Owens is and the significance of his triumph over Adolf Hitler in 1936, one could see the importance of this moment. To relegate him to the category of just being a Black sprinter and deny him his Black manhood is problematic. It highlights the way Black men are conveniently used via their

DOI: 10.4324/9781003409441-5

accomplishments (or their data and statistics) but ignored altogether when an opportunity to give them praise is apparent.

The commercial was framed in such a manner that had a Black female narrator highlighting the accomplishments of two Black women in the Olympics, implying that those accomplishments represented Black womanhood. What was suspect about this was the mention of Owens without mentioning his name, playing a very short clip of him running, but then denying him his accomplishments and his gender. However, what is further a problem is that the company behind this commercial, Verizon Xfinity, is demonstrating its investment in Black women on a corporate level. But no such investment in Black men exists. This series of investments made only in Black women while ignoring Black men remains constant. Corporate notions of diversity tend to not include Black men. This is ironic considering that Affirmative Action began with an emphasis on Black men and providing them employment since the 1970s. What has occurred instead is a hyper-investment in both white and Black women.

This commercial represents *flat blackness*. Essentially, the idea is to collapse blackness and all its subsequent demographics to highlight only one aspect of it. In the last couple of decades, that has tended to be Black women. To advance them, it has become convenient to sideline, downplay, or outright ignore Black men altogether—except when it's useful to include them in some way, shape, or fashion.

The concept of *flat blackness* comes out of the ADOS Foundation, an organization for the movement for reparations to descendants of those of African descent enslaved in North America. Founders Yvette Carnell and Antonio Moore often discussed the concept in relation to lineage on YouTube. They discussed the way lineage has often been used against blackness in the United States. Universities, for example, will emphasize increasing the number of Black students while subversively decreasing the number of African Americans. This often has to do with African Americans' reputation for protest. Thus, switching out African Americans for immigrant Black people has been a useful strategy.

However, this text uses the term *flat blackness* differently. The term specifically relates to the misuse of Black males' statistics, stories, and experiences to benefit other demographics, most particularly women and girls, in ways that do not actually benefit Black men and boys. This is a purposeful act by corporations, Black feminist academics, and media producers to obscure the historical reality of Black male vulnerability while transferring the social equity of those experiences to women. This sleight-of-hand as it relates to historical accuracy is one that Black feminists are known to use.

*Flat blackness* can come from academic, corporate, or media sources as well. When it occurs, the issue is often how much silence there is around it. An example of *flat blackness* from a news media source would be an article published last year on the current fentanyl epidemic in the Black community.

The article simply refers to an impact on the Black community despite the fact that those most-often dying from fentanyl overdoses have been Black men. The title of the article, "Black Americans bear the brunt of fentanyl 'epidemic' in Washington" (France, 2022), obscures reality by giving the focus to "everybody," again to imply that this happens equally across the board. Yet neither Black children, teenagers, women, lesbians, transgenders, nor any other demographic is dying to the extent that Black men are, but many fear pointing it out because it is considered uncouth to do so.

Recently, there has been a slew of articles dealing with suicide amongst the youth in the Black community. This is mainly because, across races and ages, women tend to attempt suicide in much higher numbers. But men tend to complete suicide in much higher numbers. Such is also the case for Black youth. But it is not just youth who are committing suicide, but particularly Black males. The obscuring of this to include every other group gives the impression that this is happening to the same extent. Much like the Twitter post in the previous chapter, where the Black woman economist in question would only point out unemployment as it related to women and teenagers while refusing to acknowledge that Black men had the worst rates for any single demographic, all these examples of *flat blackness* prevent us from identifying who actually needs structural support. These obscured realities tap dance around issues to extend a sort of social currency to a variety of demographics and sidestep the reality of who needs policy-based support most. It is not a question of winning the "oppression Olympics" or downplaying other Black demographic issues. It has to do with allowing data to point us to who is in a vulnerable position and needs help. It should be a practical engagement, and it really should not have to require fracturing into micro-demographics to solve problems. But the competition for resources brings this whole issue about.

Unfortunately, we are in an era where identifying specific demographics is key to getting structural support. And if you refuse to do so you may find that the resources you raise and the attention you gather can easily be usurped by other demographics for purposes unrelated to your initial request. This was the problem with Ferguson, Missouri. In Ferguson, residents were attempting to call attention to police abuse and police homicide against Black people (and particularly Black males) as the death of Michael Brown so poignantly highlighted. By the end of it, the focus was on a wide variety of issues. But after the spectacle of seeing a dead Black man lay in the middle of the street for hours on end, there has still been no policy change of any significance to protect the very demographic highlighted regarding police homicide in Ferguson.

Part of the problem is that much of this intraracial gender tension around activism is rooted in competition over profit and filtered through capitalism. Because of this, organizations led by Black women are competing with Black men for resources. This is often a one-way competition, as many Black men are not competing at all. This is a form of necrotic envy, a chronic form of envy produced by Black women competing for resources by performing a sort of *flat blackness* designed to increase social access. The marker of this type of gesture is the use of Black male death to gain attention, then bait and switch to other issues. After all, Black Lives Matter, despite all its public work advocating for Black male victims of police homicide, was not developed for Black men. A 2017 article has redacted the following statement from BLM co-founder Opal Tometi: "Contrary to the widely held misconceptions that Black Lives Matter was founded solely for men or boys . . . Alicia Garza, Patrisse Cullors, and I created Black Lives Matter for Black women!" (Chason, 2017; Johnson, 2018). Based on this statement it may be that their goal was to use murdered Black men for the political advancement of Black queer women.

Another example might be Black feminist Kimberle Crenshaw's organization the African American Policy Forum (AAPF), named in a manner that downplays its feminist posture. The AAPF is a group that advocates for Black women's rights under the guise of "African American policy." Their mission is noble, but its tactics are problematic and somewhat deceptive. On their website, the statement is clear: "BLACK WOMEN ARE KILLED BY POLICE TOO (AAPF, 2023)." It extends out of the popular Black feminist argument that murdered Black men use up too much attention, leaving out Black women. And although this may feel the case for some victims, it provides a logic for organizations attempting to secure more philanthropic resources. This is most assuredly what Tommy J. Curry meant by "the attempt to make attention outweigh death" (Carnell, 2017).

The "fact" section of one of AAPF's online visual advertisements for the first event of "*#HerDreamDeferred*, an Online Series on the Status of Black Women: #SayHerName: Toward a Gendered Analysis of Racialized State Violence" states,

> Myth: Black women are not foregrounded in the movement to combat police violence because they are not targets of police abuse.
>
> Fact: Police killed 313 Black men *and* women in 2012. In 2014, we collectively rallied around Black men and boys, while remaining relatively silent about Black women who are also killed that year including Tanisha Anderson, Michelle Cusseaux, and Gabriella Navarrez.

With this schoolyard-level shaming tactic, Crenshaw and the AAPF are attempting to make several subtle arguments. First, it implies that Black men are not returning the favor of supporting Black women to the same degree on the issue of Black women who have died. The question is framed in a manner that, if challenged, places one in the position of being a misogynist who hates Black women. Second, it supports the subtle idea that the number of people killed is the same across gender.

The issue here is that barring accidental deaths of Black women in the report they cited for 2012, 301 out of the 313 Black people killed in 2012 were Black males. To be clear, anyone killed unjustly in the Black community should be acknowledged, but these kinds of tactics are manipulative. There are issues in our communities that should be important to all of us while acknowledging that some issues are more germane to certain demographics than others. Running single-parent households on a relatively low income is more of an issue Black women face (empirically speaking). Those who die most due to breast cancer tend to be Black women. No one would argue anything different, but the equivalent of Crenshaw's argument would be a rally held to acknowledge "Black breast cancer survivors" but only celebrating the 2% of Black men who have died due to breast cancer as opposed to the 98% of Black women. Such would be a gross misrepresentation of the reality of breast cancer and an underhanded attempt to gain attention (and most likely resources) at the expense of those who truly die more due to the disease.

Deaths at the hands of police are an issue that overwhelmingly impacts Black males. To point that out does not diminish the deaths of Black women, which do deserve attention and advocacy. Might it be that these tactics are only used on issues that are more likely to garner philanthropic support? Does Crenshaw argue for Black men to be better represented as it pertains to single fathers and how much public aid does not acknowledge them? Instead of clouding such issues, such issues should be argued empirically and transparently.

*Flat blackness* can also occur from institutions and not just individuals. A 2018 study focused on college counselors' treatment of Black applicants at historically and predominantly white institutions. According to them,

> Most historically and predominantly white institutions (HPWIs) now desire some number of Black students on their campuses. However, recent theoretical scholarship suggests that HPWIs' desire for and willingness to embrace Black students is predicated on their racial palatability. The theory of intraracial discrimination stipulates that white gatekeepers are increasingly inclined to screen Blacks to "weed out" those they perceive as too concerned with race and racism.
>
> (Thornhill, 2019)

The study suggested that there was a problem with intra-racial discrimination in that they discriminated against anti-racist (meaning pro-Black) activists over other types of politically active (or non-politically active) Black students. They created four types of fictional students, each with male and female versions and distinctly Black-sounding names, each with very particular political ideologies. The students were either "non-descript" regarding having no activist associations, environmental sustainability activists, racial unity activists who "didn't see race at all," or pro-Black antiracist activists.

The article lamented how white male counselors seemed to discriminate against Black women antiracist activists by responding least to them when they were racial activists—6+ points less than the males. However, what I found most glaring was that counselors (both male and female) more consistently discriminated against Black males than females across the board. Across the entire chart, there was a sort of chivalry extended to girls by both sets of counselors (with women counselors often extending it more to female students than male counselors). In fact, although white male counselors responded least to Black women activists, they discriminated against Black males to the greatest degree amongst the population that they approved of most by an 18-point disparity ("environmental sustainability" activists). At no point was there even mention of a racial-gender difference in the lack of attention Black males consistently received, except to state (in only one sentence) that "As it concerns student gender, Black female students were significantly more likely than Black male students to receive responses to their inquiries irrespective of counselor gender and narrative type" (Thornhill, 2019).

No matter what Black males did, they were responded to less than their female counterparts—sometimes by a large margin, yet in the one instance where they were not, the author hyper-fixated on it and ignored the rest of the data to highlight racial sexism against Black women. That he was oblivious to the more widespread intersectional sexism against Black males provides women with more analyses that support more policy development for their advancement. The males, however, remain background noise. It is an example of *flat blackness* in the sense that the study sought to study how "Black students" were treated but then fixated on the disparities against Black females. Males' numbers contributed to the overall point that Black students were discriminated against, but the degree to which Black males were more consistently (and in a more widespread fashion) discriminated against was overlooked to foreground Black women, a gesture that has political ramifications in terms of philanthropic support and policy formation.

## II. Flat Maleness

*Flat maleness* has become somewhat popular since the 1960s. With the rise of feminism and the courting of Black women by white women within the movement, the notion of applying a white gender war paradigm to the Black community has never made much sense. The idea of "fighting the patriarchy" as it pertains to Black men has always had questionable foundations, as there has not seemed to be a period of structural Black male patriarchy of which to speak. Patriarchy is not individual acts of intimate partner violence. Nor is it anecdotal stories about fabricated anecdotes about Black men eating the big piece of chicken at the dinner table (Young, 2017). This popular cultural approach to defining patriarchy has fueled misunderstandings of its definition. Often loosely defined as a system where men hold power over women, traditional definitions were more nuanced. Errol Miller defined patriarchy as

> the term conveniently used to describe society organized on the basis of kinship, gender and age. The patriarchal society is one in which the basic unit of society is the kin group—the collective of blood-bonded individuals. This kin group can vary considerably in size and structure from the nuclear family, to the extended family, the clan, the tribe, the caste, or the race. Within the collective of blood-bonded individuals, final authority is vested in the elder males—fathers. The elder males in whom final authority is vested are not only related by blood to all members of the kin group, but are bonded to them by a system of reciprocal rights, duties and obligations.
>
> (Miller, 1988)

This text argues, generically speaking, that patriarchy is a structural system of white male privilege where power is reserved for men, but women and families benefit through male chivalry. Predictably, there is a bifurcated approach to defining patriarchy for Black men and white men. When asked early in the semester, my students define patriarchy as it pertains to white men. They articulate statistics about everything from real estate ownership to the number of male CEOs and high-level positions. They speak of structural advancement and exploitation of poor women by wealthy white men. But when it comes to Black men, they are not able to point to structural resources that Black men levy against Black women or the family. Instead, you get stories about them either engaging in individual acts of intimate partner violence or eating the biggest piece of chicken.

Nevertheless, as it pertains to patriarchy, the idea of fighting it is taken from the white community to the Black and is an example of *flat maleness*. As Black men do not share the historical lineage, status, or exploitive capability of white men, the assumption that they must be the focus when it comes to eliminating patriarchy is almost laughable. Examples of *flat maleness* are when you hear about arguments regarding fighting the patriarchy that somehow include poor Black men. In other words, arguments that "men have oppressed women since the beginning of time" (a popular feminist refrain) are a clear example of *flat maleness*.

When you address men in relation to their class standing, their historical narratives, their status in society, their poverty levels, their experiences with abuse, or their experiences with social alienation, all highlight the degree to which Black men are not white men. And neither, for that matter, are Asian, Hispanic, or Native American men. This lack of nuance, as it pertains to this so-called fight against the patriarchy, has blurred the lines between how different types of men are not white men (it is likely that even white men are not the white men they imagine). But more than just the flattening of manhood is the problematic interpretation of how to confront patriarchy. The problem has been the assumption that to attack and alienate men is to confront it, missing the point that Black men are not the ideal patriarchs they envision. Thus, when

Black men are attacked publicly for things that white men do, such nuances are usually played down.

So we have a sort of elementary idea that whatever white women take issue with white men about, Black men must be accused of the same. And this has become such a popular trope that you have activists and scholars who invoke these ideas, even though they themselves have not seen Black men commit these acts. Many are willing to transition these ideas from the academy to media based on what is taught in college classrooms and treat it as truth. In such fashion, the Academy is the biggest purveyor of *flat maleness* in that when it comes to the idea of fighting patriarchy, the treatment of all men as white men has stood in place of actually assessing men's behavior and participation in society on its own merits.

*Flat maleness* can also happen passively where data concerning Black males can go misunderstood. In other words, when data about boys and men is presented, especially in cases where Black males fare worse than others, it can go unobserved. For example, regarding young men and grading in schools, "New research from the University of Georgia and Columbia University published in the current issue of Journal of Human Resources suggests that it's because of their classroom behavior, which may lead teachers to assign girls higher grades than their male counterparts" (Weeks, 2013). Economist Christopher Cornwell observes:

> The skill that matters the most in regards to how teachers graded their students is what we refer to as 'approaches toward learning.' . . . You can think of 'approaches to learning' as a rough measure of what a child's attitude toward school is: It includes six items that rate the child's attentiveness, task persistence, eagerness to learn, learning independence, flexibility and organization. I think that anybody who's a parent of boys and girls can tell you that girls are more of all of that."
>
> The study analyzed data on more than 5,800 students from kindergarten through fifth grade. It examined students' performance on standardized tests in the categories of reading, math, and science. They then linked test scores to teachers' assessments of their students' academic progress. The data show "that gender disparities in teacher grades start early and uniformly favor girls. In every subject area, boys are represented in grade distributions below where their test scores would predict.
>
> The authors attribute this misalignment to what they called non-cognitive skills, or "how well each child was engaged in the classroom, how often the child externalized or internalized problems, how often the child lost control and how well the child developed interpersonal skills." They even report evidence of a grade bonus for boys with test scores and behavior like their girl counterparts.

> The trajectory at which kids move through school is often influenced by a teacher's assessment of their performance, their grades. This affects their ability to enter into advanced classes and other kinds of academic opportunities, even post-secondary opportunities," he said. "It's also typically the grades you earn in school that are weighted the most heavily in college admissions. So if grade disparities emerge this early on, it's not surprising that by the time these children are ready to go to college, girls will be better positioned.
>
> We seem to have gotten to a point in the popular consciousness where people are recognizing the story in these data: Men are falling behind relative to women. Economists have looked at this from a number of different angles, but it's in educational assessments that you make your mark for the labor market," Cornwell said. "Men's rate of college going has slowed in recent years whereas women's has not, but if you roll the story back far enough, to the 60s and 70s, women were going to college in much fewer numbers. It's at a point now where you've got women earning upward of 60 percent of the bachelors' degrees awarded every year.
>
> (Weeks, 2013)

The problem with their assessment is that later, they attribute this difference between how boys and girls approach education to how historically women have been discouraged from participation in the labor force. They then go on to say that they do not know how to combat this discrepancy. Although they do acknowledge this might have something to do with the fact that most elementary school teachers are women, that is where they end. So essentially, research shows that boys are being graded against a curricular standard established by using girls as a model by which to measure all children's learning. That this discounts how boys learn differently and thus hinders them early on from competing in the educational market is ignored and under-theorized upon.

This represents *flat maleness* in the sense that boys are being measured against girls and summarily dismissed early on as a demographic across race and class. And Black boys are even more ignored except for their disciplinary record, for example, and are far more handicapped by these practices than wealthier white boys. Either way, it still has a dramatic impact on their learning, their confidence, and their capacity to attend college and comparable numbers. But the point of importance here is that *flat maleness* reveals how boys are underserved, and most especially how much more detrimental these practices are for Black boys over time. One of the reasons this is considered acceptable by some is because the idea that males have been privileged in education since time immemorial justifies the contemporary one-sidedness of the benefits to (Black) girls in education, but in order to apply this logic to the

Black community one would have to prove when this time period was where Black boys were privileged academically.

Unfortunately, these ideas were wholesale appropriated into the Black community, and the gender dynamics of white society were assumed to accurately reflect the gender dynamics between Black males and Black females. Due to this lack of critical analysis, the practice of punishing Black males for being white males has become somewhat standardized, especially in fields such as Africana Studies and Women & Gender Studies.

An example of this would be the *New York Times* bestseller *So You Want To Talk About Race*, by Ijeoma Oluo. She states in her discussion guide section under "basic guidelines," "Be aware of who in the group is given the most space to talk and try to center the conversation around voices of color—and, in particular, non-male voices of color" (Oluo, 2019). She addresses how meetings should take place when issues of diversity are discussed and assumes that non-males should be able to speak more frequently than males because of this legacy of white male patriarchy. Many such feminists assume Black men have not only benefited but have mimicked these patriarchal practices. Although Tommy J. Curry used historical examples to debunk Black male mimesis in his book *The Man Not* (2017), too many of these ideas persist and are presumed to be true without evidence. (Strangely, it is somehow believed that when biological males no longer have penises, they are then somehow void of this idea of mimicry and fantastical privilege and worthy of human dignity).

## III. Black Andromortality

The actual status of Black male mortality can be better understood by stepping outside of *flat blackness* and *flat maleness*. Black men can be more accurately studied by not having the Black male plight wedded to attempts to prove other groups' vulnerability and worthiness of philanthropy, alongside not having Black men merged into this amorphous category of 'male.' After exploring the various ways Black men find themselves structurally vulnerable, it is important to analyze how this vulnerability impacts Black male mortality.

The concept of *Black andromortality* helps illustrate how Black men die far more than others in too many contexts by accounting for it across a wide variety of metrics. What becomes apparent after thorough research is that Black men are generally vulnerable in terms of mortality across the board and that this is a consequence of the societal and structural vulnerability they face. The degree to which Black men's deaths exceed Black women's across many metrics is also evidence of structural underdevelopment. Such study examines the preponderance of increased Black male death across (but not limited to) life expectancy, heart disease, cancer, homicide, COVID-19, suicide, child fatality, homelessness mortality, police homicide, intimate partner homicide, and opioid fatalities, just to name a few. Sadly, in too many areas, the medical industry does not know why Black men are more vulnerable. Some of it has to do with access to healthcare, while other aspects deal with a systemic disregard for Black male life. In either context, an important point of concern is that the vulnerability Black males suffer from in society adversely impacts them in lethal ways.

According to the National Center for Health Statistics, National Vital Statistics System, and the Centers for Disease Control and Prevention, between 1999 and 2020 about 20,000 more Black men than Black women died due to heart disease and about 40,000 more due to malignant neoplasms. More Black women tend to die due to cerebral vascular disease, diabetes, and Alzheimer's Disease. (It should be noted, however, that these three diseases impact them more over the age of 65, and it could be argued that too few Black males live long enough, hence the increased elder Black female mortality.)

In terms of the top ten causes of death, homicide and HIV make the list, but not for Black women. In fact, in terms of suicide, 4,473 Black females have died from 1999 to 2020, while 29,735 Black males have. Regarding HIV, 30,799 Black women have died in contrast to 76,946 Black males. According to the CDC's New HIV Infections by Race and Transmission Group, in terms of HIV infections, about 2,500 drug users per year are infected. Among heterosexual men, 450 are white, 530 are Hispanic/Latino, and 1,400 are Black/African American. Among heterosexual women, 930 are white, 1,000 are Hispanic/Latino, and 3,100 are Black/African American. Among gay and bisexual men, 5,100 are white, 7,900 are Hispanic/Latino, and an incredible 8,900 are Black/African American! (New HIV Infections Disproportionately Affect Black Gay and Bisexual Men and Black Heterosexual Women, 2019)

In terms of homicide, 21,424 Black females have died; in contrast, 165,606 Black males have. The disparities in death rates between Black men and Black women are palpable. According to the Centers for Disease Control and Prevention and the National Center for Health Statistics, between the ages of 10 and 14 and 20 and 24 is when Black male death skyrockets. It reaches 100.6 per 100,000 between the ages of 20 and 24, while for Black women the same age range yields a percentage of about 10.6 per 100,000 (Homicide Rates by Race and Gender, 2020).

The point here again is not to suggest that Black female lives matter less. It is to suggest, however, that because Black males are dying to a much greater degree in terms of homicide and HIV, there is something about their lives that should be analyzed, studied, and supported that much more. In essence, why are they dying more? More to the point, contrasting Black males and females highlights that some issues are not just Black issues but are particularly Black and male issues, an approach that should be a part of the intersectionalist approach to analyzing Black males' quality of life, but it only seems to work for Black females.

This is what complicates movements like *#SayHerName*. The hashtag presupposes that most people know about the Black males who have died or been killed in some way shape or form. Most people do not. When it comes to police homicide, for example, most people may be aware of one or two names from the last three to five years (especially if they died on camera), but many of them go ignored annually. It is not to say that we should not focus on murdered young women but that we need to do so in a manner that does not blame murdered Black males for being responsible for either their own deaths or others' lack of attention. Generally, the case is that too many Black men die, and that is not a direct threat or attack on Black women, nor should it be treated as such.

### *Life Expectancy*

In terms of life expectancy, women generally live longer than men. According to the CDC's National Center for Health Statistics, Black men have the lowest life expectancy at birth and at age 65. According to economist Richard Reeves, white women's life expectancy at birth is 81.3 (years old), but at age 65 their life expectancy goes up to 85.5 (Reeves et al., 2022). Black women, at birth, have a life expectancy of 78.5 years old, but by the time they are 65 it goes up to 84.6. White men, at birth, have a life expectancy of 76.6, but at age 65 it goes up to 83. Lastly, Black men have a life expectancy of 72 at birth, and by age 65 it goes up to 81.4. It has gone up over the years (in 1970 life expectancy was 60 years old), but according to the data on life expectancy by 2015, they still had the lowest numbers (Murphy et al., 2013).

Other sources present the data differently. Between 1900 and 2021, white men's life expectancy went from 46.6 to 73.7 years old, white women's went from 48.7 to 79.2, Black women's went from 33.5 to 74.8, and Black men's went from 32.5 to 66.7 years old ("Black Life Expectancy," CDC). In fact, life expectancy has dropped for most since 2014. White men's went down by less than three years, white women's went down by about two years, Black women's went down by about four years, and Black men's dropped by about six years since 2014!

What should be noted, however, is that during the pandemic (from 2020 to 2021), Black men were the only group who lost three years off their life expectancy. As noted by *The Grio*,

> Black men's loss of 3 years of life expectancy since the onset of the pandemic is comparable to the average American's loss of 2.9 years in World War II.
>
> While 1.8 years is significantly less than the 11-year loss in life expectancy following the 1918 influenza pandemic, the decrease due to COVID-19 was especially difficult for marginalized populations—and even more specifically, Black men, who died at rates greater than any other

racial or ethnic group. In the first six months of 2020, Black men's life expectancy decreased by 3 years. This mirrors the 2.9-year life expectancy loss the average American experienced during the height of World War II. At the same time, white people have collectively experienced a loss of 1.2 years of life expectancy during the pandemic.

(Benbow, 2022)

### *Cancer*

In terms of cancer, the CDC determined that Black men in 1999 had death rates at 350 per 100,000. By 2011 their death rate had lowered to about 260 per 100,000 as far as "All Cancers Combined" across ethnicity, race, and sex than for any other demographic of males. The highest rates beyond Black males' were somewhat of a tie between white males and American Indian/Alaskan natives. In comparison, Black women's rates for "All Cancers Combined" ranged from 200 to 180 per 100,000 from 1999 to 2011 ("All Cancers Combined, Death Rates by Race/Ethnicity and Sex, U.S., 1999–2011"). They, too, outrated white and American Indian/Alaskan Native women by at least 30 per 100,000. In other words, Black men had the absolute highest mortality rates in regard to all cancers combined by far until 2011.

The latest data from the American Cancer Society suggests that there has been a reduction (thankfully) in cancer death rates (Cancer Mortality Continues to Drop in Females as Breast Cancer Reversal Looms, 2022). From 2016 to 2020, Black males were the second-highest cancer rate victims, just under American Indian and Alaskan natives at 216 versus 216.5. Still, their cancer rates were much higher, as Black women's rates were 149.2 (Statista, 2023). Furthermore, Black men are more likely to develop prostate cancer compared to Caucasian men and are nearly 2.5 times as likely to die from the disease. Although scientists do not yet understand why prostate cancer incidence and death rates are higher among African American men, it is widely believed that it is a combination of genetic differences, lifestyle, nutritional habits, and lack of medical care that may all play a role in the statistics.

### *COVID-19*

Although *Black andromortality* is about paying attention to the death rates of Black men across different contexts, the issue of COVID-19 forces us to examine the role of *necrotic envy* in some Black feminist circles. In an article written by Andrea Blackstone in 2021 entitled, "Black women are dying of COVID-19 at higher rates than men and other racial/ethnic groups" she wanted to highlight how much more Black women were dying than "men." She states, "Black women have COVID-19 mortality rates that are almost 4 times higher than that of white men and 3 times higher than that of Asian men, as well as higher than white and Asian women." She also briefly notates that "the disparity in mortality rates between Black women and white women is over 3 times the disparity between white men and white women." And "the disparity between Black men and Black women is larger than the disparity between white men and white women." What was most striking however was, nestled in the data, where she stated, "Black men have far higher mortality rates than any other sex and racial group, including over 6 times higher than the rate among white men" (Blackstone, 2021).

One would think that this article would be about the demographic dying to the greatest degree. Especially considering that not a lot was being written about Black men at that time, it would have been welcome new information. But the politics behind why this was being written could be figured out fairly early on, as it talked about this being new information from a paper in the *Journal of General Internal Medicine* published by the GenderSci lab at Harvard University. The GenderSci lab's focus was to publish the first analysis of sex disparity in COVID-19 mortality while emphasizing the specific vulnerability of Black women. The problem was they discovered the vulnerability of Black men, and since men have a gender you would think that that would be sufficient. It appears that COVID-19 was so bad that it alone was the reason for the loss in three years of Black male life expectancy (Santhanam, 2021).

### *Suicide*

In terms of suicide, Black males' rates have been staggering, especially for the last 30 years. According to the American Association of Suicidology:

- In 2006, 1,954 African Americans completed suicide in the U.S. Of these, 1,669 (85%) were males (rate of 8.8 per 100,000). The suicide rate for females was 1.4 per 100,000.
- In 2006, there were only 285 African American female suicides. The ratio of African American male to female suicides was 5.85 to 1. The suicide rate among African American females was the lowest of all racial/gender groups. For African American youth, the rate of male suicide (4.34 per 100,000) was 5.1 times higher than that of females (0.85 per 100,000).
- As with all racial groups, African American females were more likely than males to attempt suicide, and African American males were more likely to complete suicide.
- From 1981 to 1994, the suicide rate increased 83% for 15–24 year-old African American males and 10% for African American females. Since 1994, the rates for males have decreased 67% for males and 23% for females.
- Males accounted for 90.5% of African American elderly (65 and older) suicides.

("African American Suicide Fact Sheet," 2006)

The rates have been skewed for years, not just between the Black community and the white community, but also between the genders intraracially. In essence, the common trope across all races is that women attempt suicide in much higher numbers than men, but men complete suicide in much higher numbers than women. This is especially so for young men, but it is also the case for elderly men as well. Nevertheless, the rate of Black male suicide has continued to increase for decades. Plainly put, suicide is gendered and raced. That being the case, if we applied a truly intersectional approach to this dynamic, Black males would find themselves the subject of intense scrutiny. Unfortunately, we are in an era where focusing on men and boys is considered inherently misogynistic. This, unfortunately, leaves many Black men and boys ignored in terms of the severity of suicide and the intense need for resources toward stemming its tide.

Suicide rates for Black males have been going up since 1981, but they have gone up another percentage since 2013. Rajeev Ramchand, Joshua A. Gordon, and Jane L. Pearson observe that

> the suicide rate increased for Black male youth in this age group by 47%, from 12.2 per 100 000 individuals in 2013 to 17.9 per 100 000 individuals in 2019.
>
> (Ramchand et al., 2021)

Sometimes the rates are so astonishing that they are hard to comprehend. At times the rate has been over a 100% increase (and not only suicide but sometimes the injury that can result from the attempt).

> According to a recent report, the *Centers for Disease Control and Prevention* (CDC, 2020) indicates that suicide is the third leading cause of death for Black [males (ages 10–34)] in the United States. When examining rates of suicide among Black youth by gender, 164 adolescent females and 609 adolescent males died by suicide in 2017 (Curtin & Hedegaard, 2019). Between 1991 to 2017, suicide rates increased by 73% for Black youth, and injury by attempt increased 122% for adolescent Black males (Lindsey et al., 2019). This would suggest that Black males are engaging in more lethal means when attempting suicide.
>
> (Brady et al., 2021)

The latest data is no better, and without a significant push to change this practice, all indications suggests that this is targeted to get much worse.

> New data show a nearly 80% increase in Black male adolescents attempting suicide since 1991. Suicide ideation has also increased, particularly for white, Black, and Hispanic women.
>
> (Sandoval, 2021)

> And
>
> Black (79.7% increase; 95% CI, 0.1%–1.5%) adolescents had greater increases in the prevalence of suicide attempts.
>
> (Xiao et al., 2021)

Put another way,

> Researchers are sounding the alarm about the number of young Black men who are dying by suicide. A report published by the Centers for Disease Control and Prevention showed that although the overall rate of suicide in the United States decreased by 3% in 2020 (the latest year stats are available), the rate of suicide actually increased among many men of color, including Black men, who according to the Suicide Prevention Resource Center, have a death rate from suicide three times greater than for Black women.
>
> The study found that Black males had the highest increase in suicide attempts compared to any other race in the group, for example, increasing nearly 80%.
>
> (Tate, 2023)

### *Homelessness Mortality*

But suicide also blends into other issues. For the sake of further exploring *Black andromortality*, homelessness mortality, as it relates to race and gender, is quite alarming. According to the National Alliance to End Homelessness and the National Health Care for The Homeless Council there are distinct characteristics to the majority of America's homeless (State of Homelessness, 2022). Most individuals tend to be Black (by the percentage of their total population), male, and older. They also have distinct characteristics in how they tend to die.

The greatest population to die is 408,891 individuals between 2007 and 2020. This is followed by 171,575 families, and then the 110,528 "chronically homeless individuals." Veterans are at about 37,252 deaths, and 34,210 were unaccompanied youth. In terms of "Counts and Rates by Gender" as of 2020, 352,211 of the male homeless population and 223,578 of the female homeless population died. Transgender deaths were 3,161 and non-binaries were at about 1,460. Racially, the predominant population of homeless is white at 280,612, but the second-highest population is Black at 228,796. It is important to remember that the Black community is only about 13% of American society. To be the second-highest population of homeless suggests that Black people find themselves vulnerable to greater degrees than even whites, particularly when unhoused.

The majority of the unhoused tend to be older men in their 50s and 60s. Journalist Thomas Fuller of *The New York Times* observes:

> More than ever it has become deadly to be homeless in America, especially for men in their 50s and 60s, who typically make up the largest cohort of despair. In many cities the number of homeless deaths doubled during the pandemic, a time when seeking medical care became more difficult, housing costs continued to rise and when public health authorities were preoccupied with combating the coronavirus.
>
> The process of tallying homeless deaths is painstaking, involving the cross-referencing of homeless databases and death reports. But based on data from the handful of California's 58 counties that report homeless deaths, experts said that 4,800 is a conservative estimate for last year. In Los Angeles County, the homeless population grew by 50 percent from 2015 to 2020. Homeless deaths have grown at a far faster rate, an increase of about 200 percent during the same period to nearly 2,000 deaths in the county last year.
>
> (Fuller, 2022)

But as the homeless are difficult to track, much of which is done by volunteer account, the estimates of deaths range. So though there may be debate about how many homeless there are, there is little debate about how many of the dead are predominantly male. According to the National Health Care for the Homeless Council,

> The estimate of 5,800–46,500 deaths among people experiencing homelessness per year highlights the vast, and largely hidden, scale of homeless deaths in the U.S.
>
> Men account for approximately three in four of homeless decedents. In Austin, Texas, 87% of people who died while experiencing homelessness were male, compared to 13% female. The proportion is lower in some places, such as Multnomah County, Oregon, where 76% of homeless decedents are male and 24% are female. Only San Francisco, California, reported homeless deaths for transgender individuals (<1%) and no city or county recorded homeless deaths for non-binary individuals.
>
> Black people (who, along with Indigenous people, are most impacted by homelessness in the U.S.) constituted the next largest group [after whites] in many places, from 6% in Santa Clara County, California, to 38% in Philadelphia. In Santa Clara County, Latinx people made up 31% of homeless decedents.
>
> (National Homeless Mortality Overview, 2020)

Causes of death were difficult to ascertain, as many of these are inconsistently reported. Still there were some overarching findings:

- Natural and accidental deaths: In Denver, 33% of deaths were due to natural causes and 47% due to accidents.

- Substance use disorder: New York City, 32% of deaths were due to substance abuse.
- Trauma and violence: Multnomah County found 11% of deaths were due to homicide and 10% due to suicide. Los Angeles County found 24% of deaths were due to trauma or violence.
- Cardiovascular disease: In New York City, 28% of homeless deaths were attributed to cardiovascular issues (National Homeless Mortality Overview, 2020).

Although it is difficult to find rates of homelessness by race, gender, and sexuality, what we can glean from these data is that most of the homeless are individuals, the second highest population (by number) of homeless are Black (highest by ratio-to-population size), they tend to be older, and they and tend to be male. That said, the quintessential homeless person in America tends to be an older Black male on the streets by himself. They tend to be the most vulnerable in terms of death and tend to be the most isolated. Keep in mind that there are only 50,000 fewer Black homeless than white, nationally speaking. This means that if Black America was the measurement for homelessness, comparatively speaking, only a fraction of them are (as it should be) homeless. For Black America, this is not the case.

### *Child Fatalities*

In regard to child fatalities, journalist and associate professor Stacy Patton of Morgan State University sums up this author's opinion quite well when she states:

> Reading the latest Annual Child Maltreatment Report, which I do each year when they are released. The latest numbers on child fatalities by race and ethnicity shown below are for 2019. I went back 10 years and calculated the number of fatalities for Black children. Between 2009 and 2019, a total of 4,298 Black children died as a result of maltreatment. Black children are killed at a rate of 2 to 3 times higher than their white counterparts. Around 40% of the fatalities were a result of hitting children. Boys make up the larger proportion of victims and women are the primary perpetrators.
>
> When it comes to the calculus of Black life, I often see many debates that focus on the murders of Black men, Black women, Black trans women and arguments about who is killing who more. And we SHOULD be talking about the causes and consequences of these lost lives. But meanwhile, folks do not talk about the fact that each year an average of around 430 Black children are killed in our communities.
>
> (Patton, 2021)

Like the homeless, there are distinct characteristics as to which children tend to die. Predominantly, the majority are under 1 year old. They tend to be male by a child fatality percentage of 60.1% in contrast to females at 39.5%. And again, much like homelessness, even though African American child fatalities are second to white child fatalities numerically, the child fatality percentage is much too close for a population as small as the Black community. For 2020, there were 560 white child fatalities and 504 African American child fatalities. The fatality percentages were at 38.7% to 34.9% respectively. The difference is clearer when regarding the child fatality rate per hundred thousand. Whites were at 1.9 and African-Americans 5.9. So again, whites had higher numbers, but Black people had a higher rate based on population size.

The dominant forms of child maltreatment were neglect, physical abuse, and medical neglect. Such issues are mostly environmental, as they are related to poverty and drug and alcohol use. Perpetrators of maltreatment of Black children also have characteristics. They are predominantly between the ages of 18 and 44, mostly white (with the second-highest population of Black people at 48.4% and 20.8% respectively). Perpetrators also tend to be parents, and mostly female (i.e., mothers).

According to a chart on "Child Abuse Fatalities And Perpetrators By Gender Among African Americans All U.S. States Within D.C. And Puerto Rico From 2015 to 2020" by the National Data Archive on child abuse and neglect, NCANDS child file, the total number of Black child fatalities in 2020 were 3,146 (data gathered by Stacey Patton, Twitter, March 28, 2022). Black male victims were at 1,812, and Black female victims were at 1,334. In terms of perpetrators, Black male perpetrators were at 1,692, while Black female perpetrators were at 2,106. Put another way, in terms of rates, Black male children suffer death at the greatest rates mostly by neglect (including medical neglect), psychological maltreatment, and physical abuse. To be clear, these issues are not a product of inherent malice. They are a product of a social ecology of Black America rooted in poverty, drugs, alcohol, and unemployment. Still, it is important to note that in that dynamic, Black boys seem to suffer fatality at a greater rate than others, suggesting that this starts at a young age.

Stacy Patton discusses child fatality in a sadly unique manner by contrasting it with police homicides of children (data gathered by Stacey Patton, Twitter, March 4, 2023). A chart she makes sourced by *The Washington Post's* "Fatal Force" police shooting database, 2013 through 2018, and the ACF annual child maltreatment reports, 2013 and 2018,points out that between those years Black children were killed in far greater numbers by parents than by cops (Child Maltreatment, 2020). In 2013, she says 7 kids were killed by police officers, but 375 were killed by parents. In 2014, the numbers were 5 to 359. In 2015, 5 to 368. In 2016, 6 to 401. In 2017, they were 12 to 416. And in 2018, the numbers were 6 to 470 for a total of 41 children killed by police and 2,389 killed by parents. When applying the ratios from the maltreatment report, 2020, it is believable that the majority of these children killed by both police and parents were likely Black and male.

### *Police Homicide*

As far as police homicide is concerned, Black men die 20 to 30 times more often than Black women. Many see the random and even state-sanctioned murders of Black males and boys as something to overlook, an opportunity for other demographics to use as a talking point, or as a social good (*state-sanctioned* refers to how few police get punished for their crimes). Clearly, none of these areas is embraced overtly, but the absence of widespread support for the lives of Black males, the lack of new policy designed to protect Black male lives, and the infrequency with which police officers receive jail time for killing Black males suggest that such issues are dubiously supported.

Approximately 200–300 Black males are killed per year by police officers, and about 9–13 Black females. More specifically, according to *Guardian.com* in 2015, 295 Black males and 12 Black women were killed by police violence. In 2016, 253 Black males and 13 Black females were killed in 2016 (Swaine et al., 2022). According to *The Washington Post*, 214 Black males and 9 Black women were killed by police in 2017. In 2018, as of October 1 when the page was last updated, there were 183 Black men and 7 Black women killed by police (Fatal Force: 2018 Police Shootings Database, 2020. Also see Washington Post, 2022).

The limited awareness of many of these Black males killed per year reflects their invisibility. Even amongst anti-police brutality activists, the names of (maybe) five Black males received repeated attention, and those are often males killed in past years. The reality of the 200–300 Black males killed annually is generally disregarded when the issue is brought up formally in media. Such rates are only matched by Native Americans. Political groups have used Black male deaths as a talking point to increase their profile, but often the conversation will quickly shift to other demographics. For example, with Black Lives Matter, the organization brandished the injustice of the deaths of young men such as Michael Brown but quickly shifted much of its attention to Black women, LGBTs, and even Black girls while advocating for families—often without acknowledging Black men as fathers. In typical Black feminist fashion, such has continued since the death of Michael Brown, and Black men are even subtly blamed for taking up too much attention because they die too much (Beckett & Clayton, 2022). Yet even when such deaths are reported, the fact that the emphasis is placed on a given Black male's criminal background highlights the subtext of the reporting—that is, that he deserved to die and is no longer a threat to the public. Yet despite the reasoning, the deaths of Black males at the hands of police continue.

*Table 4.1* Police Homicide in the Black Community by Race and Gender (2015–2023)*

| | | | | |
|---|---|---|---|---|
| 2023** | 1 | Black Women | 24 | Black Men |
| 2022 | 9 | Black Women | 214 | Black Men |
| 2021 | 9 | Black Women | 224 | Black Men |
| 2020 | 2 | Black Women | 240 | Black Men |
| 2019 | 6 | Black Women | 230 | Black Men |
| 2018 | 10 | Black Women | 219 | Black Men |
| 2017 | 9 | Black Women | 214 | Black Men |
| 2017 | 13 | Black Women | 253 | Black Men |
| 2015 | 12 | Black Women | 295 | Black Men |

*Source:* *According to *A National Epidemic: Fatal Anti-Transgender Violence in the United States in 2019*, 3% of the 20–26 actual transgender homicides (across races) per year are police homicides. The *Human Rights Campaign* reports that "15 trans people have been killed by police or while incarcerated in jails, prisons or ICE detention centers since 2013."

**Data in 2023 up until April 6, 2023.

Although each demographic in Table 4.1 can claim that their murders are underreported, the ratio of deaths holds consistent.

According to the National Epidemic Fatal Anti-Transgender Violence in the United States, about 3% of total transgender homicides across race per year are police homicides (see *Report: A National Epidemic: Fatal Anti-Transgender Violence in America in 2019* and Report: *An Epidemic of Violence*, 2020). This usually translates to about one every few years. Furthermore, "Transgender people of color account for 81%of known victims this year, and 59% were Black. Trans-women are disproportionately represented, as they have been in years past, also comprising 81%of the deaths recorded at the time of publication" (Schoenbaum, 2022). This suggests that the overwhelming majority of transgendered persons killed annually were born biologically Black and male. This is distinctly different from the experiences of most transgendered persons biologically born female. Such suggests a unique form of anti-Black misandry in that much of the hostility that leads to fatalities extends to a very distinct group.

### *Opioid Fatalities*

Some of the latest data to shock the world has been about the opioid fatalities Black men face at disproportionate degrees. The current opioid epidemic, generally associated with white suburban life and spurred on by fentanyl, has managed to reflect the heightened state of vulnerability that other areas reveal when regarding Black males: they are dying too much. According to a 2022 study in the *Journal of the American Medical Association* entitled, "Disparities by Sex and Race and Ethnicity in Death Rates Due to Opioid Overdose Among Adults 55 Years Or Older, 1999 to 2019,"

> During the period 1999 to 2019, 79,893 U.S. residents 55 years or older died due to an opioid overdose. Among these individuals, 79.97% were aged 55 to 64 years, and 58.98% were men. Annual numbers of deaths increased over time from 518 in 1999 to 10,292 in 2019. Annual rates of opioid overdose deaths per 100,000 persons 55 years or older increased over time and ranged from 0.90 in 1999 to 10.70 in 2019. Substantial variation by sex and by race and ethnicity was found. In 2013, rates among non-Hispanic Black men began to diverge from those of other demographic subgroups. By 2019, the opioid overdose fatality rate among non-Hispanic Black men 55 years or older was 40.03 per 100,000 population, 4 times greater than the overall opioid overdose fatality rate of 10.70 per 100,000 for persons of the same age.
>
> (Mason et al., 2022; Johnson, 2022)

PEW Research Center data even suggests that between 2015 and 2020, death rates for opioid overdose were dramatically different than assumed, even between Black men and women. Black women's rates went from 7.7% to 18.8% by 2020, while Black men's went from 17.3% to 54.1% (Gramlich, 2022). Again, such data does not suggest that one group should be ignored, but it may suggest that this is not necessarily just a Black issue, but more so a Black male issue.

# Part II

# Solutions

## The Black Masculinist Turn in Action

# 5 The 17-Point Black Male Political Agenda

## A Solution

This text posits that *The Black Male Political Agenda* is a consequence of the Black masculinist turn. In essence, these 17 points are a product of frustrated Black men, many of whom have concluded that the policies that have shaped the Black community over the last century have worked to their disadvantage. They began to call for policy changes that better work in their interests. Strangely, this was influenced by feminism. After the rise of both feminism and Black feminism in the 1960s through the 1990s, Black men, for the most part, still maintained a 1970s-era notion of blackness, the sense of community that shaped their political worldview. However, with the rise of Black feminism, in particular Black women's interest in developing their own politic, their own resources, and their own relationships to the State (spurred by welfare practices and other such policies outlined in the first chapter), Black men have only recently decided they needed to articulate their own political interests. In interviews they have had over the last few decades with presidential candidates, for example, few could articulate Black male political interests with specificity. This contrasts with many Black women, who could both articulate the needs of their own demographic and that of the community (or at least maintained a need for women to do so). With the rise of social media, Black men have started to publicly reflect on the lack of interest the community itself seems to have in their political input and their diminished voting capacity via carceral disenfranchisement. Couple this with how they have been perceived and treated in mainstream culture, and it is becoming painfully clear to them that not having a racial and gender-specific focus has only worked to their detriment.

*The Black Male Political Agenda* began in 2020 on T. Hasan Johnson's YouTube show *The Onyx Report*. In the three years since, supporting subscribers listed at nearly 35,000 on YouTube, 5,000 on Facebook, and 6,000 across three Twitter accounts, and none of that includes the support from The Onyx TV Network at *https://onyxchannel.network/* and The Institute for Black Male Studies at *www.instituteforblackmalestudies.com/* (with its corresponding YouTube page). And still, that does not even account for other content creators' willingness to incorporate *The Black Male Political Agenda*

DOI: 10.4324/9781003409441-7

onto their platforms (channels such as "BGS IBMOR," "The Green Gorilla," "Dr. Ronald Neal," "Doctor Thunder," and "Artisan MC," just to name a few). That said, well over 100,000 self-identified Black men online have some connection to the agenda itself via subscribership and views.

The movement began as a call for Black men to start to think about policies that would benefit them. The number of suggestions began slowly but then quickly rose to 17 points within two years. Despite those suggestions that could come from anyone whose ideas benefitted Black men and boys, most contributors were Black men. The website for the agenda can be found at *Black Masculinism And New Black Masculinities* at *https://newblackmasculinities.wordpress.com/2020/09/24/the-black-male-political-agenda-by-t-hasan-johnson-ph-d/*. On the web page for the agenda, one can see only one disclaimer: "It is believed that the ideas proposed here should identify the target audience when drafted into policy: Black males. It should be made unapologetically clear that these are not just for people of color, the poor, etc. In essence, this list is meant to be an archived compendium of policy ideas designed to improve Black males' collective quality of life."

The agenda is a living document with a static webpage available for any to make suggestions and send in their thoughts as comments. As more and more Black men began to participate, the list expanded with a specificity commensurate with the unique niche areas of Black male life. Thus, ideas ranged from family court reform to homelessness programs to data disaggregation to law enforcement and more. Black men from all walks of life contributed ideas about what would improve their ability to participate in society on an equal footing with others not underdeveloped in a similar fashion. It is presented here in the order it organically developed from items 1 to 17.

This book was influenced by two separate movements that only have loose associations through random individuals and stemmed out of different discourses. The general movement of men that I refer to is only evidenced by the various groups that seem to, on one level or another, advocate for (Black) men. As those groups formalized, they begin to develop very different value systems, but the main components of shared interest have remained in men's lives. There has been an online movement of men since at least 2010. This movement has been slowly growing and has been pushing men to reflect on their station in life and articulate their thoughts about it. Depending on how far back you choose to go, you can find remnants of larger grassroots male movements. These movements, going back to at least the 1970s had stunts and starts and may have only advanced one another indirectly. Nevertheless, they have grown into a crescendo on many disparate fronts. Some of these movements have no direct correlation with one another while others seem to evolve out of their predecessors. Black men created separate online spaces (one such space is Black Mansophere 1.0), only to be joined later by Black men who were once MGTOWs ("Men Who Go Their Own Way," a group of mostly white men who abstain from playing socially expected male gender roles) but who left due to white racism.

The Black "Manosphere" 2.0, developed by Mumia Obsidian Ali, Juan "The Angryman" Valdez, and Oshay Duke Jackson on YouTube and other social media platforms has seen involvement by men of a wide variety of backgrounds, coming together organically to articulate their interests. Many Black men have not had a widely accessible public platform to speak, dissimilar from what was offered to Black women via Black feminism since the 1980s. This author's interest in the Black Manosphere is rooted in its possibilities. It is a unique opportunity to study Black men in that this space is comprised of men who range from poor to wealthy, have an expanded geographical locale, and live a variety of lifestyles from intensely single (monkhood) to long-term marriage. These men range the gamut in terms of occupation. Some are doctors, lawyers, professors, and other types of white-collar Black elites, while others are blue-collar workers such as truck drivers or retail workers. Others are entrepreneurs building their own businesses, whether they are just starting out with one employee or are quite successful making anywhere from six to eight-figure annual incomes. Such a wide variety of these men not only constitutes this space but has contributed to the list of policy ideas proposed in this chapter.

Black Male Studies, on the other hand, developed in the late 2010s under the direction of Tommy J. Curry and his publishing of *The Man Not: Race, Class, Genre, and the Dilemmas of Black Manhood* (2017). The field's endeavor is an extension of earlier periods of Black scholars advocating for Black males. This discourse has primarily taken place in the academy, with periodic involvement by individuals, organizations, and institutions interested in working with and for Black males. As Black males have begun to publish and research more in this area, there has been a growth in Black male scholarship, but as there is still only one formal department in Black Male Studies at the University of Edinburgh, Scotland, the field is still in its early stages.

Nevertheless, those who contributed to the development of *The Black Male Political Agenda* hailed from both groups, the Black Male Studies group and the Black Manosphere group. They contributed annotated suggestions with linked websites and even personal anecdotes about why these contributions or policies are necessary. It is not to say it is the only conceivable solution for the plight of Black men in America, but it is to say that a shift in policy would be advantageous because many of the conditions that Black men experience were shaped by policy in the first place. Furthermore, generations of one-sided policies have worked against Black males and are further deeply entrenching negative attitudes about Black men. This, in turn, has even influenced how Black males have been raised from boyhood by internalizing negative perspectives about them buoyed by policy. So, it stands to reason that correcting this would require a shift in policy and will likely need two to three generations to take effect.

There are many other ideologies that offer a range of alternatives to improve the Black community's situation from spiritual detachment from materialism to revolution, from conservative cultural movements to a call for deep investment in the American political system. This text does not argue that policy is a better or worse solution than those other options. It merely suggests that policy is one such useful option.

Some of the contributors to this list have opted to stay anonymous for fear of retribution against their livelihood. Others who have asked to be acknowledged are doing so under the guise of online titles. This is consistent with the culture of Black men's online content creation (especially in the Black Manosphere). Arguably, this may be one of the reasons Black men have not spoken up in widespread fashion regarding some of the identitarian and gender-based theoretical trends of the last few decades, many of which were hostile to them analytically and professionally.

Lastly, it should be noted that the discourse, proposals, and even the citations used throughout the agenda itself are all based on freely accessible information, reiterating that this is a product of a grassroots movement. From the use of YouTube, WordPress, *BlackDemographics.com*, and Wikipedia to specific contributors' own knowledge from experience or occupation to online content creators creating their own research, this list of policy proposals comes directly from the very Black males people need to hear from. One of the primary differences between these groups and groups such as Black feminists is that neither group focused upon here has been sponsored by any major institution, corporation, organization, or government. As a result, *The Black Male Political Agenda* is an unsponsored grassroots idea (except for private micro-donations from online subscribers).

Special thanks to contributors to this list "BGS IBMOR," "Adam IBMOR," Attorney Dennis Spurling, "David W.," "Stuart K.," "Tristan J.," "Bryan M.," "Chief in the South," "Charles F.," "AAI," "Lamont 2X," and Douglass Jefferson (Senior VP of *The National African American Gun Association*).

## STREAMLINED LIST:

1. Family Court Reform (16 subpoints)
2. Education (3 subpoints)
3. Affirmative Action for Black Men
4. Targeted Homelessness Programs
5. Targeted Unemployment Programs
6. Criminal Law Reform and Law Enforcement (12 subpoints)
7. Intimate Partner Violence/Homicide Policy Reform (3 subpoints)
8. Health: Targeted Treatment and Recognition for Heart Disease, Cancer, Suicide, and HIV Campaigning (4 subpoints)
9. Targeted Small Business Support
10. Social Security and Life Insurance Family Support
11. Paternity Leave

12. Reverse Voter Disenfranchisement
13. Black Male Specific Reparations for the Trans-Atlantic Slave Trade Through 21st-Century Hyperincarceration (3 subpoints)
14. The United Nations: We Charge the U.S. With the Genocide of the Black Male
15. Title VII Reform
16. Data Disaggregation
17. Black Men's Rights to Self-Defense

## DETAILED LIST

1) Family Court Reform

Referencing issues discussed in Chapter 1, the Family Court's treatment of Black men has unfairly and drastically diminished Black men and boys' quality of life by privileging women as the primary caregivers.

a) *Child Custody*

1. This includes automatic 50/50 child custody as long as fathers can prove what mothers are required to as far as being able to provide a stable and safe living environment. Once determined, pre-existing income-based alimony/child support judgments levied against Black men should be re-assessed. Also, child support payments for either parent should be eliminated with 50/50 custody and should only be considered if there isn't a 50/50 custody arrangement.
2. The presumption of law that 50/50 custody is in the best interest of the child or children. Child support is only available where 50/50 custody has not been awarded (Dennis Spurling).

b) *Mandatory Paternity Testing at Birth*

Before signing the birth certificate, newborns should be given a DNA test to ensure the father's parentage, thus avoiding men being unjustly responsible for supporting children under false pretenses. This should be REQUIRED before any issuance of child support judgments.

***Addendum A:***

Once determined that the father has been misled regarding the child's parentage (no matter how long it has been), he should be excused from both the birth certificate and child support (at his determination). The exploited party should be subject to legally sanctioned reimbursement from the mother, the biological father, and relevant city/state/federal government offices. Interest should be 7% (compounded annually) in addition to the principle owed to the injured party. Furthermore, the "Presumption of fatherhood" should be formally stricken as established law.

c) *Reinstituting AT-FAULT Divorce Standards*

In alignment with gynocentric family court policies, no-fault divorce negatively impacted Black men by authorizing a massive shift in marital culture that dramatically underdeveloped them economically (Adam IBMOR).

d) *Termination of Parental Obligation*

As we understand the law, it is a woman's right to choose whether or not she will carry a baby to term, put the child up for adoption, or abort it. Therefore, within the first 6 months of being informed about the pregnancy, men should have the right to financially disassociate themselves from it. (Formerly "*Financial Abortion.*" Term renamed by YouTuber "*Hoodservative*.")

Also, we should automate financial abortion for cases of "female stealthing" (when a woman sabotages male contraception) and criminal charges should also be added (Adam IBMOR). (See Browne, 2022.)

e) *Child Support Value System*

We advocate instituting a system where goods, services, and time spent with a child should be calculated and valued at a dollar amount (any remaining deficit to be paid in cash). Also, child support should be capped at $2,500 per child regardless of income (except in the case of suggested practice addressed in the letter "i" that follows). (Spurling, 2021.)

f) *Right-to-Lifestyle*

Post-divorce, men should be entitled to the life they have been accustomed to in marriage. Thus, any judgment or consent determination must ensure that the husband can enjoy the same privileges and lifestyle enjoyed BEFORE or DURING the marriage, whichever costs more to maintain (Adam IBMOR).

g) *Require Formal Child Support Management Reports*

Ensure those child support payments are explicitly earmarked for approved child-related expenses only. Costs used on non-child-related expenses must be accounted for by the custodial parent. (Xavier B.)

h) *Prohibit Jailing for Failure to Pay Child Support*

Such incarceration frequently punishes men for being poor more than anything else. This, in turn, increases Black male unemployment and further hurts families' economic stability. (Tristan J.) ("Child Support and Incarceration," 2023)

i) *Income Floor for Child Support*

1. There should be a set minimum income for anyone on child support.
2. If someone is chronically under this floor in terms of income, state governments should provide opportunities for them to intern at an apprenticeship in a trade.

3. Only if they quit and refuse to work in an apprenticeship should they be incarcerated (BGS IBMOR).

j) *Child Support and Alimony Assistance Program*

Where it can be proven that a man's child support and alimony judgment requirements are causing a practical impact on his standard of living, the state government and municipality shall pay the cost in whole or in part (but no less than 66%) of the total cost of the child support and alimony payments. (Adam IBMOR)

k) *Tax Filing Options*

At income tax time, it is believed that some women "sell" their children's social security numbers to friends, family members, etc.; either when the mother is not working or has maxed out her two-child benefit to receive income credits. Thus,

1. Whenever a third party submits tax returns claiming care of another person's child, any child support orders to the mother of the stated child should be rendered void. (Or denial of the third party's claims on the child as a dependent. This should fall under saving tax dollars.) The natural question should be, *Why is the mother being paid for a child under the care of third party?*
2. Welfare benefits and incentives for women fuel the single-mother phenomenon. So, to eliminate welfare contingencies (or to incentivize contingencies for fathers), we propose a cap on subsidizing single mothers and/or subsidizing single fathers.
3. Any child support paid should be considered earned income (due to taxing it). Women can claim child support as an extra earned income that improves their credit and ability to finance vehicles and other products and services. Men who pay child support are not allowed to claim payments made when filing taxes, even when the amount can be a third to even 50% of their earned income.
4. We advocate a policy that exempts child support payments from the applicant's gross income when they apply for public housing and or housing assistance. The payment is counted as income for the custodial parent and counted in the gross income for the non-custodial parent; their gross income dictates their acceptance into the program and their rent amount. Some men may not qualify due to their gross income being over the limit, but they may not actually bring that amount home due to child support payments. His rent may be exceptionally higher since H.U.D. states that 30% of gross income should go to rent. This leads to a plethora of issues for many brothers in the community such as Black male homelessness,

joblessness, and the propagation of children born out of wedlock. ("Chief in the South")

5. Amend Title IV(D) of the Social Security administration code granting states matching funds up to 66% of what they recover from persons who have committed paternity fraud and collected child support and arrears, and other state and federal benefits. (Dennis Spurling)

l) *Revising the Child Support Formula*

Child support is treated as another form of alimony, so two things should be addressed by the Family Court (nationally):

1. Fifty-fifty custody should eliminate child support (assuming expenses are jointly paid by both parents).
2. The formula that determines child support is predicated on an outdated model of women not working. Now that labor participation is fairly equalized in terms of gender, the notion used by some states of children requiring 25–50% of parent's income should also be paid in equal measure by both parents—but:
   a. men's majority child support default status where men are the secondary parent needs to be re-assessed (see *The Tender Years Doctrine*), and
   b. the 25–50% child support for men required to pay it (who do not have 50/50 custody) should have their payments pro-rated to a percentage-based judgment against her (usually ignored) labor.

m) *Child Support and D.N.A. Testing*

There should be mandatory D.N.A. testing before the granting of child support orders (Dennis Spurling).

n) *Eliminate the Suspension of Driver's Licenses and Passports*

No state should suspend someone's driver's license and passport for failure to pay child support. All states have statutes to suspend someone's license for failure to pay child support. Juxtapose this to 17 states that allow unauthorized immigrants to apply for a driver's license.

Suspending someone's driver's license, especially a Black man's, prevents him from earning a living. This, in turn, makes life more difficult when many undocumented immigrants are able to get driver's licenses to pursue those very jobs Black men may have lost due to such punitive practices (AAI).

o) *Child Support as a Trust Fund*

The family court should determine that a small percentage of child support should be required to be put in a trust for the child to be made available to them at age 18 (DJ Vlad, 2022 at 3 min).

p) *Nullify Family Law's Criminal Court Behavior*

Criminal allegations are to be heard in criminal court. Domestic violence and child abuse are crimes listed in the criminal code and as such those alleged of these crimes are to be afforded all the procedural and substantive due process protections associated with the 14th Amendment to the United States Constitution. Family "law" courts are not the proper venue for mediation of criminal matters. It is customary in the Family law setting for private attorneys to act as special prosecutors against private citizens and prosecute criminal allegations. This is a blatant perversion to the course of justice and creates obvious impediments to fairness. Family "law" court IS NOT a court of law. It is a court of equity, and there are some stark differences between the two. Essentially, a private attorney can prosecute you for criminal allegations of child abuse and/or domestic violence in Family Court, robbing you of your rights to a speedy jury trial and a criminal attorney (Lamont 2X).

2) Education

Referencing issues raised in Chapter 1, educational institutions play a huge role in influencing Black boys and men from preschool through graduate school. Yet the discrimination and underdevelopment they experience at the hands of teachers, practices, the administrative bureaucracy, and educational policies do a great disservice to the supposed mission to educate Black males.

a) *Single-Sex Pedagogy and Institutions*

As there is documentation to suggest that Black boys perform better in all-male environments(particularly under male teachers), it is proposed that boys be educated in environments that are all male, preferably Black, and rooted in a pedagogy that seeks to improve their performance by prioritizing their history, culture, and gender.

b) *Preparatory Reading/STEM Educational Support*

Ten percent of city, state, and federally targeted resources for incarceration should be diverted to educational afterschool programs for ADOS/FBA boys. Even funds earmarked for special education can be used to draft male college-level teaching assistants to create an all-male educational support structure. Also provide tax breaks for private companies who may philanthropically donate materials, tech, etc. Lastly, cable/internet companies are incentivized by federal/tax policy to provide free high-speed internet.

c) *Single-Sex Education*

Should include curricula that accommodate the learning style of young boys. Rote learning styles may be insufficient, and tactile styles of learning may need to be implemented for them. In later years of schooling, financial education for Black boys should be a requirement.

3) Affirmative Action for Black Men

Double minority status for Black males where they have access to employment and higher payment income floors based on their race and gender. This is in response to generations of policies that disproportionately disadvantaged Black males based on their race and gender—most particularly Affirmative Action practices from the 1980s onward that prioritized white women and Black women over Black men.

We propose that Black men be offered permanent government employment at $25/hr. (with the bi-annual cost of living increases and pay increases depending on the type of job) and then after high school graduation, the successful completion of the G.E.D. (General Educational Development Test) by the age of 18 (however, if one graduates early but is at least 16, they must be emancipated from their parents). Such employment should include on-the-job training and one should be vested after 30 years. Once vested, if one chooses to continue working, their employee retirement contribution will then go into a personal retirement fund. Based on Black men's life expectancy (66 years [rounded down] by 2021–see graphic in #8), the job should come with a post-retirement pension after at least 35 years of employment—but one's pension should not be received until the age of 58. If one is deceased before age 58, a portion (40%) of their pension should be designated to a declared beneficiary (inspired by Prof. Irami Osei-Frimpong and BGS IBMOR).

4) Targeted Homelessness Programs

Referencing issues raised in the discussion on Black andromortality, especially post-incarceration, Black men should be prioritized for housing as they are most often turned away despite having housing vouchers. Consequently, as Black America constituted half of America's homeless (pre-COVID), and remains disproportionately homeless, the majority of the homeless (across races) tend to be male. This makes Black males the most susceptible group to homelessness.

5) Targeted Unemployment Programs

As Black males experienced unemployment at rates over 40–50% in over 34 major cities before COVID, many need advocacy and policy that prioritizes their employment on both racial and gendered grounds (Cherry, 2016).

6) Criminal Law Reform and Law Enforcement

Law enforcement has historically barred Black males from justice, while at times being the source of injustice for Black men.

a) *Criminal Sentencing Reform*

Black men should be arrested and sentenced to no greater degree than any other members of any race who commit the same crimes as per the chart "Women of All Races Get Shorter Sentences Than White Men," organized by

*FiveThirtyEight*, U.S. Sentencing Commission. According to the presented data, no race of women experienced sentencing more than white men at any point between 2000 and 2016 (Dagan, 2018).

According to the "Average Sentence for white Male and Black Male Offenders Fiscal Years, 1999–2016," U.S. Sentencing Commission, 1999–2014, the average sentence of white men has been between 40 to 60 months, but Black men were sentenced between 65 to 85 months (Average Sentence for White Male and Black Male Off enders Fiscal Years, 2016).

> Black male offenders continued to receive longer sentences than similarly situated white male offenders. Black male offenders received sentences on average 19.1 percent longer than similarly situated white male offenders during the Post-Report period (fiscal years 2012–2016), as they had for the prior four periods studied. The differences in sentence length remained relatively unchanged compared to the Post-Gall period.
>
> Violence in an offender's criminal history does not appear to account for any of the demographic differences in sentencing. Black male offenders received sentences on average 20.4 percent longer than similarly situated white male offenders, accounting for violence in an offender's past in fiscal year 2016, the only year for which such data is available. This figure is almost the same as the 20.7 percent difference without accounting for past violence. Thus, violence in an offender's criminal history does not appear to contribute to the sentence imposed to any extent beyond its contribution to the offender's criminal history score determined under the sentencing guidelines.
>
> Female offenders of all races received shorter sentences than white male offenders during the Post-Report period, as they had for the prior four periods. The differences in sentence length decreased slightly during the five-year period after the 2012 Booker Report for most offenders. The differences in sentence length fluctuated across all time periods studied for white females, Black females, Hispanic females, and Other Race female offenders.
>
> (Demographic Differences in Sentencing, 2017)

b) *Licensing Law Enforcement*

Law enforcement professionals have a revocable license that can be permanently stripped to keep them out of the profession like lawyers, doctors, etc. Police are protected under the ruling of police protection from incriminating information or keeping their job. (David W.)

c) *Proxy Violence*

Proxy violence should be recognized as a criminal offense, punishable by no less than 50% of the primary offense prison time. (Adam IBMOR)

d) *End "Qualified Immunity"*

Often negotiated into union contracts, qualified immunity is a legal principle that grants government officials (especially law enforcement) performing discretionary functions immunity from civil suits unless the plaintiff shows that the official violated "clearly established statutory or constitutional rights of which a reasonable person would have known."

e) *Jury Nullification*

> Jury nullification (U.S.) generally occurs when members of a criminal trial jury believe that a defendant is guilty, but choose to acquit the defendant anyway, because the jurors consider that the law itself is unjust, that the prosecutor has misapplied the law in the defendant's case, or that the potential punishment for breaking the law is too harsh. *Some juries have also refused to convict due to their own prejudices in favour of the defendant.*
>
> (Wikipedia, 2023)

Jury nullification disproportionately affects Black men. Thus, 30% of the jury should be Black men. More specifically, when a Black man has to go before a jury, 30% of that jury must be of his Black male peers.

f) *False Accusations*

There should be clear and more stringent punishments for filing false charges against Black men. Knowing that Black men are denigrated, stereotyped, and wrongfully convicted more than (and to greater degrees than) others, such accusations can have a more far-reaching and detrimental impact on Black men's lives. Black men are the most exonerated group due to false accusations according to the National Registry of Exonerations (Race and Wrongful Convictions In the United States, 2017), University of California Irvine. They state,

> African Americans are only 13% of the American population but a majority of innocent defendants are wrongfully convicted of crimes and later exonerated. They constitute 47% of the 1,900 exonerations listed in the National Registry of Exonerations (as of October 2016), and the great majority of more than 1,800 additional innocent defendants who were framed and convicted of crimes in 15 large-scale police scandals and later cleared in "group exonerations."
>
> (p. 1)

Thus, whimsically dangerous charges with questionable/unreliable evidence (or no evidence at all) should be harshly dealt with to dissuade others from repeating this action against an already vulnerable population.

g) *Minimum Age of Criminal Responsibility*

The minimum age of criminal responsibility in the U.S. should be raised to at least 18 years of age. Most states do not have a lower age limit to where a person can be charged, prosecuted, sentenced, etc. for a statutory offense. The states that do specify an age floor, mostly range between 7 to 10 years of age. Such legal precedents contribute greatly to the criminalization of Black boys. (Tristan J.)

- www.ncjj.org/pdf/JJGPS%20StateScan/JJGPS_U.S._age_boundaries_of_delinquency_2016.pdf
- www.jjgps.org/jurisdictional-boundaries
- https://en.wikipedia.org/wiki/Age_of_criminal_responsibility#The_age_of_criminal_responsibility

h) *End Law Enforcement Collaboration*

This would prohibit state and local officers from using federal databases to search for prior criminal records when in the process of questioning or apprehending a Black male. Officers more often than not decide their level of aggression based on one's alleged prior history. There is a legislative precedent for such a law already, as California has adopted it under the designation SB54 to protect illegal immigrants. (David W.)

- Web: https://en.wikipedia.org/wiki/California_Senate_Bill_54_(2017) And here is the official legislative.
- Text: https://leginfo.legislature.ca.gov/faces/billNavClient.xhtml?bill_id=201720180SB54

i) *End Arbitrary Stop and Frisk*

Enact legislation abating the U.S. Supreme Court Case *Terry v. Ohio* 392 U.S. 1 (1968), which is a violation of the 4th and 14th Amendment and the line of cases that flow from *Terry*, id. (Dennis Spurling).

> *Terry v. Ohio*, 392 U.S. 1 (1968), was a landmark U.S. Supreme Court decision in which the Court ruled that it is constitutional for American police to "stop and frisk" a person they reasonably suspect to be armed and involved in a crime. Specifically, the decision held that a police officer does not violate the Fourth Amendment to the U.S. Constitution's prohibition on unreasonable searches and seizures when questioning someone even though the officer lacks probable cause to arrest the person, so long as the police officer has a reasonable suspicion that the person has committed, is committing, or is about to commit a crime. The Court also ruled that the police officer may perform a quick surface search of the person's outer clothing for weapons if they have reasonable suspicion that the person

> stopped is "armed and presently dangerous." This reasonable suspicion must be based on "specific and articulable facts," and not merely upon an officer's hunch.
>
> ("*Terry v. Ohio*," https://en.wikipedia.org/wiki/Terry_v._Ohio)

j) *Self-Financed Police Liability Insurance*

Require police officers to take out individual policies of liability insurance to cover intentional and negligent actions while performing their duties as peace officers, thereby holding individual officers personally accountable and limiting the exposure to money judgments the taxpayers must bear. (Dennis Spurling)

k) *Retribution for Corrupt Systemic Sentencing Practices*

Black people, Black men especially, are 7.5 times more likely to be wrongfully convicted. (Center, 2022) (AAI)

In fact,

> The report, *Race and Wrongful Convictions in the United States 2022*, reviewed the cases of 3,200 innocent defendants exonerated in the United States since 1989. Black people, the researchers found, were 7 times more likely to be wrongfully convicted, were more likely to be the targets of police misconduct, and more likely to be imprisoned longer before being exonerated.
>
> Black people were overrepresented in every category of the 1,167 wrongful murder convictions in the Registry's database. African Americans constituted 56% (74/134) of all death sentenced exonerees; 55% (294/535) of wrongful murder convictions resulting in life imprisonment; and 54% (270/497) of wrongful murder convictions in which exonerees were sentenced to imprisonment for terms of years. "Innocent Black people are about seven-and-a-half times more likely to be convicted of murder than innocent white people," the Registry reported. That figure, the report noted, "applies equally to those who are sentenced to death and those who are not."
>
> (Center, 2022)

In essence:

- The federal government incentivized cities and states to write more strict laws and build more prisons. The states also proceeded to write more strict laws and build more prisons.
- For-profit private prisons contract with State governments to keep prisons at least 90% full.
- Judges sentence innocent people or levy excessive felony sentences against plaintiffs for minor crimes and misdemeanors while collecting kickbacks.

- Prosecutors brag about high prosecution rates, often orchestrated by offering plea deals with sentences that are excessive in punishment.
- Expert testimony is used to convict innocent people.

As a consequence of this dynamic, state and federal governments should have to pay $1 million per year to any Black man who is exonerated of crimes he didn't commit. For-profit private prisons should have to pay the exonerated 10% of the prisons' revenue (not profits) for every year the exonerated was in their prison. Also, prison executives and investors should be liquidated of their ownership of the prison and sentenced to 25 years to life. Judges should be disbarred, sentenced to 25 years to life, and have to pay damages of $150,000 to the exonerated. Prosecutors should be disbarred and have to pay damages of $150,000 to the exonerated. Expert witnesses hired by the prosecutors should lose their professional license, be barred from court proceedings, be sentenced to 25 years to life, and have to pay damages of $150,000 to the exonerated.

l) *Government Investment in Black Male-Centered Diversion Programs*

Both state and federal governments should increase investments in diversion programs whereby Black male youth/men will be able to participate at a rate proportionate to their representation in the crime to which they have been found guilty of committing. For example, if 70% of assaults in Black communities were committed by Black males, then 70% of the participants in related diversion programs should be Black male youth/Black men.

7) Intimate Partner Violence/Homicide Policy Reform

Despite stereotypes that intimate partner violence/homicide aggression is the sole purview of Black males, it is nigh equal (bidirectional) in the Black community (meaning men assault women to the same degree women assault men, and the numbers of intraracial IPV homicide amongst the 40+ million Black population is negligible), with data suggesting that women (across race) initiate violence first, while opting to use weapons more often than men.

a) *Abolishing the Duluth Model*

> The Duluth Model is the most common batterer intervention program used in the United States. Critics argue that the method can be ineffective as it was developed without minority communities in mind and can fail to address root psychological or emotional causes of abuse, ***in addition to completely neglecting male victims and female perpetrators of abuse.***
>
> (Wikipedia, 2023) (Adam IBMOR)

More than ignoring male victims, the Duluth Model proposed that men were de facto guilty of being the primary abusers of women whenever a woman experienced some form of intimate partner violence. It ignored women's greater capacity to initiate violence and/or be aggressors of IPV.

b) *Intimate Partner Violence-related Carceral Practices*

Black men incarcerated for IPV require a massive re-evaluation of their status regarding their victimization at the hands of women. As rates of bidirectional abuse in the Black community suggest equal violence initiated by women to men (w→m) and from men to women (m→w) and the *hypo-sentencing of women for the same crime as men by up to 63%*, the under-representation of female aggressors suggests a massive bias in sentencing that disproportionately targets and criminalizes men—especially when you consider the rates of violence toward men, and Black men in particular according to a meta-study of IPV data going back to the 1980s.

> This procedure resulted in retaining seven epidemiological/population-based studies with a total of 82,836 sampling units (44,930 females and 38,906 males). . . .
>
> Among those reporting IPV and using weighted averages, across these samples, 57.9% of the violence reported was bidirectional. Correspondingly, 42.1% of the violence reported was unidirectional in nature. Within the 42.1% unidirectional violence, 13.8% was coded as perpetrated only from the man toward the woman (M→F unidirectional), whereas 28.3% of the reported unidirectional violence was from the woman toward the man (F→M unidirectional). These numbers are similar to those originally reported by Stets and Straus (1989), based on their sample of 5,005 married, 237 cohabiting, and 526 dating couples. According to this book chapter, based on data collected in the 1980s, 50% of violent dating couples engage in bidirectional IPV (39.4% female-to-male only, 10.5% male-to-female only). Among cohabitating violent couples, 52.4% were classified as bidirectionally violent (26.9% female-to-male only, 20.7% male-to-female only); whereas 48.2% of married violent couples were bidirectionally violent (28.6% female-to-male only, 23.2% male-to-female only). Among the seven current large population studies that were used in this analysis, the overall ratio of unidirectional female-to-male compared to unidirectional male-to-female IPV was 2.05 weighted (2.02 unweighted ratio).
>
> (Langhinrichsen-Rohling et al., 2012, p. 208)

The chart "Table 8: Rates of Bidirectional and Unidirectional Violence Reported Among white, Black, and Hispanic Ethnic Groups From the Same Sample" shows that Black men are the most abused demographic of every group across gender and race. First, it shows that rates of bidirectional violence are higher among Black people than whites and Hispanics. Second, it shows how Black men are less violent toward their females than white and Hispanic men (and Black female-initiated violence was less than other groups of women's violence toward their men). And third, it shows that Black female-initiated violence not only exceeded Black male-initiated violence (as women were more violent than their men across race), but that the extent to which they were more violent than Black men was greater than the violence ratio between other groups of women and their men (p. 218).

c) *Sexual Assault/Rape Acknowledgment*

This includes legally recognizing the withholding of sex as a form of sexual abuse in marriage. That said, such an acknowledgment might allow for less punitive access to annulments and divorce options. (It also requires that all rape allegations require traditional standards of adequate evidence before arrest and sentencing.) (Adam IBMOR)

8) Health: Targeted Treatment and Recognition for Heart Disease, Cancer, Suicide, and HIV Campaigning

a) *Heart Disease*

Heart disease is the number-one killer of African Americans, but Black male deaths exceed Black women's, suggesting that Black males require more targeted research and treatment. According to the "10 Leading Causes of Death, United States, 1999–2020" by the National Center for Injury Prevention and Control, Centers for Disease Control and Prevention, 843,670 Black males died due to heart disease, 21,616 more than Black women for the same time period (Leading Causes of Death, United States, 2020). Prior to 2017, Black women were more susceptible to heart disease, but that year we saw a 2,000-person increase in men versus women. A year prior, that 2,000-person difference was comprised of more women than men. Six years later, that gap has expanded to over 20,000. Something is happening specifically with Black men that requires further analysis.

b) *Cancer*

Black men are diagnosed with cancer at slightly less rates than whites but die from it more than them and Black women. The scale for measuring Black male cancer is three times larger per 100K than Black women's.

> It was shocking for me to learn that African American men have the highest death rate and shortest survival of any racial and ethnic group in the U.S. for most cancers, and that prostate cancer is the number-one diagnosed cancer among veterans.
>
> (Chris Tucker, Prostate Cancer Foundation, 2019)

One out of eight U.S. men will be diagnosed with prostate cancer. In 2022, nearly 269,000 men will be diagnosed with this form of cancer, and over 34,000 will die as a result. Prostate cancer is the second most prevalent form of cancer in men. A man is more likely to develop prostate cancer than he is to develop colon, kidney, melanoma, and stomach cancers combined. While prostate cancer deaths have been reduced by more than 50% in the last three decades, the reality is still worse for African American men.

***African American men are:***

- About 75% more likely to be diagnosed with prostate cancer than Caucasian men.
- More than twice as likely to die from the disease.

(Prostate Cancer Additional Facts for African American Men and Their Families Guide, 2022)

c) *Suicide*

Black male suicide has been dramatically increasing as of late, and there needs to be targeted treatment regarding addressing this in both boys and men.

> The study, published Monday in the journal *JAMA*, found that teenagers attempting suicide increased 22% over the course of nearly three decades, but the trend varied depending on sex and race. Black males had the highest increase in suicide attempts compared to any other race in the group, for example, increasing nearly 80%.
>
> Kelsie Sandoval, "Suicide Attempts Are Rising Among Young Black Men. Experts Say They Face A 'Perfect Storm' Of Hardships," *www.insider.com/rise-young-black-men-attempting-suicide-perfect-storm-of-hardship-2021–6*. (Sadoval, 2021)

## FACTS ABOUT BLACK BOYS AND SUICIDE

- Self-reported suicide attempts for Black adolescents rose by 73% between 1991 and 2017.
- Black boys are increasingly likely to attempt suicide, while Black girls have more ideation than attempts.
- Black boys are engaging in more lethal means when attempting suicide than Black girls, which has increased by 122% between 1997 and2017.
- Black boys are twice as likely to die by suicide than white youth.

## FACTS ABOUT BLACK MEN AND SUICIDE

- In 2014, 80% of suicide deaths in the Black community were men.
- Recent research has observed that Caribbean Black men in the U.S. have the highest attempt rate for the African American community.
- Firearms were the predominant method of suicide among African Americans regardless of sex or age. Suffocation was the second-most prevalent method.

- Black men don't often recognize depression or trauma as an issue, therefore they don't associate S.I. (suicidal ideation) as a problem.
(Douglas, "Black Boys, Black Men, And Suicide")
Also, see

***African American Suicide Fact Sheet Based on 2014 Data, 2016***

- In 2014, 2,421 African Americans died by suicide in the U.S. Of these, 1,946 were male (80.38%). The overall suicide rate per 100,000 was 5.46.
- In 2014, there were 475 African American female suicides in the U.S. The suicide rate of African American females was the lowest among men and women of all ethnicities.
- In 2015, researchers released data showing that there were more suicides among African American children ages 5 to 11 than among Caucasian children. This was the first national study to observe higher suicide rates for African Americans than for Caucasians in any age group.
- While the majority of studies show that African American men are more likely to die by suicide while African American women are more likely to attempt suicide, recent research has observed that Caribbean Black men in the U.S. have the highest attempt rate for the African American community.
- The suicide rate for African Americans ages 10–19 was 3.11 per 100,000.
- For African American youth (ages 10–19), the rate of male suicides (4.60 per 100,000) was 2.9 times higher than that of females (1.57 per 100,000).
- Males accounted for 81.5% of suicides completed by elderly African Americans (ages 65+). This percentage is mirrored by the suicides completed by elderly Caucasian men.
- Firearms were the predominant method of suicide among African Americans regardless of sex or age, accounting for 47.42% of all suicides. [Between 1991 and 2017, suicide rates increased by 73% for Black youth, and injury by attempt increased 122% for adolescent Black males (Lindsey et al., 2019). (Brady et al., 2021] Suffocation was the second most prevalent method (29.9%). (African American Suicide Fact Sheet Based on 2014 Data, 2016).

Also,

Black adolescent boys are more likely to suffer from an injury due to suicide attempts from lethal weapons and suicide-related hospitalizations for Black youth have also steadily increased from 2008 to 2015 (Lindsey et

> al., 2019; Plemmons et al., 2018). This uncovering is alarming as suicide attempt is the risk factor that is most strongly associated with later death by suicide (Bilsen, 2018).
>
> (Brady et al., 2021)

In addition,

> Findings: In this cross-sectional study of 183,563 adolescents in the U.S., a decreasing temporal trend in suicidal ideation changed to an increase, with different turning points for female (2009), white (2009), Hispanic (2007), and Black (2005) adolescents. Male and Black youths had nonsignificant changes in suicidal ideation, but the greatest increase in the prevalence of nonfatal suicide attempts.
>
> Males, particularly Black male adolescents, appear to have the greatest need in terms of prevention of suicidal behaviors. Both groups have underperformed in help-seeking capacity and there may be stigma and racial barriers to getting psychiatric treatment for young Black males. Strategies that prioritize monitoring the trends in risk factors for suicidal behaviors in racial/ethnic subgroups, design culturally appropriate prevention programs, alleviate structural inequality, reduce mental health stigma and barriers to health care, and promote help-seeking should be ethnically and sexually diversified for effective suicide prevention.
>
> (Xiao et al., 2021)

And,

> This chapter examines suicide and suicidal behaviors among African American adolescent and young adult males. It shows that the odds for suicide were highest for African American males, even after controlling for the numerous clinical, geographic, and sociodemographic vulnerability factors associated with suicide.
>
> The study also confirmed prior research showing that having a gun in the home substantially increases the risk for suicide. This is particularly true for males, as illustrated by the almost fourfold increase in the risk of suicide when a gun is known to be in the home.
>
> (Joe, *Suicide Among African Americans: A Male's Burden*)

Finally,

> The study, published Monday in the journal *JAMA*, found that teenagers attempting suicide increased 22% over the course of nearly three decades, but the trend varied depending on sex and race. Black males had the highest increase in suicide attempts compared to any other race in the group, for example, increasing nearly 80%.

> Young Black men are treated as stronger and older, but don't have people to talk to about vulnerability. The study authors said young Black men face financial hardship, among other stressors, and may have untreated mental health needs.
>
> (Sandoval, 2021)

d) *HIV*

Black men, those who have sex with men to be specific, are the most vulnerable group when it comes to HIV infection and mortality. Again, targeted support is needed to stem the high rates of mortality of Black males.

> Although they represent only 12% of the U.S. population, Black people account for a much larger share of HIV diagnoses (43%), people estimated to be living with HIV disease (42%), and deaths among people with HIV (44%) than any other racial/ethnic group in the U.S.
>
> ("Black Americans and HIV/AIDS: The Basics," 2022)

Furthermore, in regard to gay and bisexual men, by 2020:

- Among gay and bisexual men, Black men have been disproportionately affected by HIV and account for 39% of HIV diagnoses attributable to male-to-male sexual contact.
- In 2018, male-to-male sexual contact accounted for more than half (59%) of new HIV diagnoses among Black people overall and a majority (80%) of new diagnoses among Black men.
- Young Black gay and bisexual men are particularly affected, with those ages 13–24 representing over half (52%) of new HIV diagnoses among all gay and bisexual men in that age group.

Change is needed to help address the alarming shift in life expectancy Black males have been facing since 2020.

9) Targeted Small Business Support

Commensurate with our status in society, and considering the lack of capital and inherited wealth, Black male-owned businesses should be targeted (particularly during COVID) for support.

10) Social Security and Life Insurance Family Support

Accrued social security and life insurance from deceased Black males should be partly applied to children and grandchildren (when applicable). (Stuart K.)

11) Paternity Leave

Federally mandated (nationally imposed) "parental leave" should be provided for fathers on a state, private, and federal level and applied nationally across the board. As Black men have been designated the most participatory fathers across race in a recent study articulated by Josh Levs in his text, *All In: How Our Work-First Culture Fails Dads, Families, and Businesses—And How We Can Fix It Together* (2015), their lack of access to parental leave is unjust.

12) Reverse Voter Disenfranchisement

Allow Black male ex-convicts to have their voting rights restored upon release from incarceration. For context, review the origins of voter disenfranchisement for convicts:

> The historical context for this comes from old English common law which justified the concept of "civil death" as punishment for conviction of treason or a felony because a person committing a crime had "corrupt blood," making the person "dead in the law." America did not immediately adopt this position because the Constitution was silent on voting rights—it neither granted nor denied anyone the right to vote.
>
> In 1787, the Constitution considered Black people as three-fifths of a human being. Blacks voting was not an issue. Then came the Civil War and the 13th, 14th, and 15th Amendments. Enslaving people, except as punishment for a crime, was illegal. Birthright U.S. citizenship was established, explicitly including freed enslaved people. Black men got the right to vote. Over 2,000 Black men were elected to government offices, and they began purchasing or homesteading property and voting.
>
> America responded. The exception in the 13th Amendment allowing slavery as punishment for a crime was paired with "Black Codes," which basically criminalized Black life. Blacks convicted under Black Code laws were leased out to do work, providing cheap labor to boost the South's faltering economy. In 1850, 2% of prisoners in Alabama were non-white. By 1870, it was 74%. At least 90% of the "leased" prison laborers were Black.
>
> In the 15 years between 1865 and 1880, at least 13 states—more than a third of the country's 38 states—enacted broad felony disenfranchisement laws. The theory was simple—convict them of crimes, strip away the right to vote, imprison them, and lease them out as convict labor and Blacks would be returned to a condition as close to slavery as possible.
>
> What is the result of this history? Black Americans of voting age are more than four times as likely to lose their voting rights than the rest of the adult population. One of every 13 Black adults is disenfranchised. In some states like Virginia, Kentucky, Tennessee, and, until recently, Florida, one in five Blacks have been disenfranchised. In total, 2.2 million Black citizens are banned from voting. Thirty-eight percent of the disenfranchised population in America is Black.
>
> (Robinson, 2019)

13) Black Male Specific Reparations for the Trans-Atlantic Slave Trade Through 21st-Century Hyperincarceration

Reparations is a crucially overlooked area that has required redress since the late 19th century. Due to the United States' treatment of Black men specifically, practices deemed legal dramatically targeted and impacted Black male life in a manner distinct from the rest of Black America altogether (see James Sidanius' work on *Social Dominance Theory* for more detail on "outgroup male treatment"). Thus, in addition to petitions for reparations for all African Americans whose ancestors were enslaved in the United States:

a) *Specific reparations should be given to Black men specifically due to:*

   1) the exclusivity of treatment from the onset of slavery to (roughly) 1800, a time period where Black males were sought after to a greater degree than even Black women for enslavement,
   2) their prioritization of lynching and terrorist mistreatment,
   3) the designation that they only were allowed 3/5th a vote when given the right, then terrorized not to even be able to use it,
   4) the targeted campaign to be brutalized and killed by law enforcement, and
   5) the target of hyper-incarceration policies from Reconstruction (convict leasing) through to the 1970s (prison industrial complex) to now.

b) *Targeted Wealth Declines*

Due to the impact of educational inequalities, neighborhood effects, workplace discrimination, parenting, access to credit, rates of incarceration, and many other factors, research has shown that Black males are more likely to experience

> race gaps in intergenerational mobility [that] largely reflect the poor outcomes for Black men. The report is another contribution to the growing literature showing that race gaps in the intergenerational persistence of poverty are in large part the result of poor outcomes for Black men. Specifically, Chetty et al. show that Black men born to low-income parents are much more likely to end up with a low individual income than Black women, white women, and—especially—white men.
>
> (Winship et al., 2018)

That said, reparations for Black males should be commensurate with what they have experienced both contemporarily and historically.

c) *Targeted For Growth*

Reparations for every Black boy born with $10,000 in an investment account. The investment included in the account should be an S&P 500 ETF or mutual fund. This account shall not be drawn upon until the child becomes an adult and has had financial training. (See McCormally, 2017.)

14) The United Nations: We Charge the U.S. With the Genocide of the Black Male

According to the United Nations' definition, and much of what's listed here, Black men have been subjugated, neglected, targeted, and killed to a great enough degree to warrant an investigation that covers both contemporary and historical mistreatment. (United Nations)

15) Title VII Reform

Amend Title VII (Civil Rights Act of 1964) by removing the addition of "sex" to the act, as it has been detrimental to Black males and by extension, Black families. The removal of "sex" from Title VII would be more in line with the spirit of the act as originally proposed in 1964 and would position both Black men and women as the rightful recipients of Affirmative Action resources and entitlements. It would also:

1. Help to close the racial wealth gap, while
2. Closing the wage gap between Black men and white men. And
3. remove the double-minority status of Black women and be fairer to Black men as far as employment (administrative, electoral, white-collar, etc.) and educational access. (Also see Tommy J. Curry, "Feminism As Racist Backlash: Understanding How the Will To Dominate Black Americans Drove the Development of 19th and 20th Century Feminist Theory" on Congressman Howard C. Smith and the feminist takeover of Title VII to derail the Civil Rights Movements' gains.)
4. This should also be used to prioritize the hiring (or acquisition) of Black males in federal/state positions (or institutions who get federal contracts or monies) such as in terms of college recruitment; but also in software/tech, retail, public schools, post office, law enforcement, military, and fire departments. (Charles F.)

16) Data Disaggregation

Black men are often statistically invisible. Without data that specifically focus on Black men (as opposed to Black people or men alone), the specific needs, support, and policy that must be met for Black men to have an improved quality of life will never happen. Further, any policy measures implemented to assist Black men (directly or indirectly) are doomed to fail without tracking the data. Only by means of disaggregating the data collected by public and relevant private entities can we be in a position to provide Black men with the quality of life they deserve. Therefore, in the interests of justice, we make the following demand:

We demand that federal and state laws mandate that data collection efforts present data in a manner that specifies results by race, gender, and even sexuality (when possible). This should include a specific Black-male category in addition to (or apart from) any aggregate data collected for the purpose of policy design, implementation, progress reporting, law design, ordinance design or any other intended (or actual) official government action or intended (or actual) large private firm actions in the interests of human rights, anti-discrimination or any other area of consideration that impacts (or will impact) quality of life of the studied populations. (Adam IBMOR)

17) Black Men's Rights to Self-Defense

Gun control has historically been used to disarm Black people generally and Black men specifically. The Jim Crow laws and Black codes had specific language on restrictions of Black gun ownership. In the modern day, there is no specific language as such, but the impacts are similar. The restrictions of gun control on access to common self-defense technology have left Black men at risk of both criminal victimization as well as increased contact with law enforcement primed to see Black men and boys as criminals often resulting in harassment, criminal records, or even death.

Additionally, conceal-carry permitting schemes have often been manipulated to deny law-abiding individuals from carrying firearms for self-defense. This is done by having hefty fees, convoluted application processes, and the need to have applications scrutinized by local law enforcement, all of which disproportionately deny Black men and boys the right to defend themselves. Lastly, restrictions on the types of firearms and their magazines' capacities presuppose that the government can predict the type of violent crime one may experience and the number of assailants that one might face, all of which disproportionately impact Black men and boys as this group of people has some of the highest rates and raw numbers of victimization of violent crimes.

Also, outlaw criminal inducement sting operations. This is where law enforcement induces their informants to spread rumors about drug stash houses with lots of money to poor Black men in hopes of them showing up to rob the house so that they can be arrested. Another type is where undercover agents offer exorbitant payouts for guns (sometimes as high as $150K). This has resulted in people buying guns legally to sell to the undercover officer which results in their arrest. Put another way, arrest people for committing verifiable crimes but stop enticing poor Black males to commit crimes they might not have ordinarily committed.

Lastly, eliminate criminal enhancements for drug possession charges while having possession of a firearm. This gives prosecutors undue leverage over defendants and disproportionately impacts Black men. Over the last 90 years, these types of charges make up over 80 percent of all federal firearms charges. Limit such criminal sentencing for use of a firearm, not just possessing them.

Remedies to this issue include:
Provide grant money to pay for:

1. a minimum of eight hours of firearms training with at least two hours of live fire with a reputable instructor to any Black male of at least 18 years of age,
2. the institution of firearms safety classes as part of the K-12 school curriculum,
3. institution of a seminar that educates on the Black tradition of arms (similar to what organizations like the National African American Gun Association (NAAGA) provide),
4. lastly, we support the abolishment of:

   a. gun ownership permits and carry permits,
   b. abolishment of magazine size restrictions,
   c. abolishment of semi-auto weapon restrictions, and the
   d. abolishment of "stop and frisk" policies.

(Douglass Jefferson, Senior VP of The National African American Gun Association)

# References

## Chapter One


A Higher Share of Black-Owned Businesses Are Women-Owned Than Non-Black Businesses. (2021, February 11). https://usafacts.org/articles/black-women-business month/

Abrams, S. (2022). Black men's agenda. *Georgia Gubernatorial Candidate Website*. https://staceyabrams.com/policy/constituent-agendas/black-mens-agenda/

Blackstone, A. (2021, April 7). Black women are dying of COVID-19 at higher rates than men in other racial/ethnic groups. *Black Enterprise*. www.blackenterprise.com/black-women-are-dying-of-covid-19-at-higher-rates-than-men-in-other-racial-ethnic-groups/?utm_campaign=socialflow&fbclid=iwar0gxcxuaurvpiv1n4tjuikyq9saxesifvmmoro7pexelcdnybrxcm7s9iw&test=prebid

Curry, T. J. (2017). *The man-not: Race, class, genre, and the dilemmas of black manhood*. Temple University Press.

David, M. (2018, July 2). *TV one set to launch network for women*. www.wbls.com/news/news-0/tv-one-set-launch-network-women

Demographic Differences in Sentencing: An Update to the 2012 Booker Report. (2012). www.ussc.gov/sites/default/files/pdf/research-and-publications/research-publications/2017/20171114_Demographics.pdf

Fast Facts: Women of Color in Higher Ed. www.aauw.org/resources/article/fast-facts-woc-higher-ed/

Gabriel, T. (2010, November 21). Proficiency of black students is found to be far lower than expected. *The New York Times*. www.nytimes.com/2010/11/09/education/09gap.html

Hansen, M., & Quintero, D. (2022, March 9). School leadership: An untapped opportunity to draw young people of color into teaching. *Brookings*. www.brookings.edu/blog/brown-center-chalkboard/2018/11/26/school-leadership-an-untapped-opportunity-to-draw-young-people-of-color-into-teaching/

HealthSherpa & By HealthSherpa. (2022, July 28). Top government benefits for low-income families. *HealthSherpa Blog*. https://blog.healthsherpa.com/top-10-government-programs-for-low-income-families/

Hill, A. (2022). In-depth: Why African American and Latino male college graduation rates are low. *ABC Action News Tampa Bay (WFTS)*. www.abcactionnews.com/news/in-depth/in-depth-why-african-american-and-latino-male-college-graduation-rates-are-low?fbclid=IwAR2AkV09-NCClS1Vn8nMEnu4XrrKo2nwt8j6jZI9I-H7FFeW6sroD5EyNxus

Ingraham, C. (2017, November 16). Black men sentenced to more time for committing the exact same crime as a white person, study finds. *Washington Post*. www.washingtonpost.com/news/wonk/wp/2017/11/16/black-men-sentenced-to-more-time-for-committing-the-exact-same-crime-as-a-white-person-study-finds/

King, M. L. (1967). *Where do we go from here: Chaos or community?* HarperCollins Publishers.

Kunjufu, J. (2020, July 29). Why are only 18 percent of black females proficient in reading? *African American Images*. https://africanamericanimages.com/why-are-only-18-percent-of-black-females-proficient-in-reading/

Kurwa, R. (2020). The newman in the houserules: How the regulation of housing vouchers turns personal bonds into eviction liabilities. *Housing Policy Debate*, *30*(6), 926–949. https://doi.org/10.1080/10511482.2020.1778056

Leader, L. W. A. (2017b, February 25). Letter: 'Sewing the seeds of distrust'. *Sioux-Falls*. www.argusleader.com/story/opinion/readers/2017/02/25/letter-sewing-seeds-distrust/98409616/

List of Current Digest Tables. (2021). *[Associate Degrees] National Center for Educational Statistics*. https://nces.ed.gov/programs/digest/d20/tables/dt20_321.20.asp?current=yes

List of Current Digest Tables. (2021). *[Bachelor's Degrees] National Center for Educational Statistics*. https://nces.ed.gov/programs/digest/d20/tables/dt20_322.20.asp?current=yes

List of Current Digest Tables. (2021). *[Certificates] National center for Educational Statistics*. https://nces.ed.gov/programs/digest/d20/tables/dt20_320.20.asp?current=yes.

List of Current Digest Tables. (2021). *[Doctorate Degrees] National Center for Educational Statistics*. https://nces.ed.gov/programs/digest/d20/tables/dt20_324.20.asp?current=yes

List of Current Digest Tables. (2021). *[Master's Degrees] National Center for Educational Statistics*. https://nces.ed.gov/programs/digest/d20/tables/dt20_323.20.asp current=yes

Mutua, A. (2013, May 16). Multidimensionality Is To Masculinities What Intersectionality Is To Feminism, *Nevada Law Journal*. Winter 2013. 341–367.

Nadasen, P. (2007). From widow to "welfare queen": Welfare and the politics of race. *Black Women, Gender + Families*, *1*(2), 52–77. www.jstor.org/stable/10.5406/blacwomegendfami.1.2.0052.

Nadworny, E. (2022, June 23). Getting a bachelor's degree in prison is rare. That's about to change. *NPR*. www.npr.org/2022/06/21/1106424742/college-financial-aid-prison#:~:text=The%201994%20crime%20bill%20signed,prisons%20offered%20higher%20education%20programs

Number and Percentage Distribution of Teachers in Public and Private Elementary and Secondary Schools, by Selected Teacher Characteristics: Selected Years, 1987–88 through 2015–16. (2017). *Digesting of Education Statistics*. https://nces.ed.gov/programs/digest/d17/tables/dt17_209.10.asp?current=yes

One Million Black Women. (2020). *Goldman Sachs*. www.goldmansachs.com/our-commitments/sustainability/one-million-black-women/

Ong, D. (2022, May 1). *Federal Pell Grants revived for prisoners after nearly three decades*. https://sanquentinnews.com/federal-pell-grants-revived-for-prisoners-after-nearly-three-decades/

Raspberry, W. (1995, February 10). Moynihan's scissors. *Washington Post*. www.washingtonpost.com/archive/opinions/1995/02/10/moynihans-scissors/cfdce49c-4707-40f2-a8ee-f2c34767d263/?fbclid=IwAR3BESfeB9djC61gBuiQadf3OiPcbx-7m_nn9w2h70QPxwTvW5SP6tUVrHk

Reeves, R. V., & Kalkat, S. (2023, April 19). Racial disparities in the high school graduation gender gap. *Brookings*. www.brookings.edu/2023/04/18/racial-disparities-in-the-high-school-graduation-gender-gap/?utm_campaign=Economic%20Studies&utm_medium=email&utm_content=255698479&utm_source=hs_email

Reeves, R. V., & Smith, E. (2022, March 9). Americans are more worried about their sons than their daughters. *Brookings*. www.brookings.edu/blog/up-front/2020/10/07/americans-are-more-worried-about-their-sons-than-their-daughters/?fbclid=IwAR0nbrDZoLLnHPTreOsZ3evq4dFLGQdq_rWbir7Xa1hpK2OtrbCqv0Ly8k4

Share, C., & CalMatters, M. L. (2017, June 5). 75% of black California boys don't meet state reading standards. *The Mercury News*. www.mercurynews.com/2017/06/05/75-of-black-california-boys-dont-meet-state-reading-standards/

Staples, R. (1972). The matricentric family system: A cross-cultural examination. *Journal of Marriage and Family*, *34*(1), 156–165. https://doi.org/10.2307/349644

Starr, S. B. (2015). Estimating gender disparities in federal criminal cases. *American Law and Economics Review*, *17*(1), 127–159. www.jstor.org/stable/24735732

Stemple, L., Flores, A., & Meyer, I. (2016). Sexual victimization perpetrated by women: Federal data reveal surprising prevalence. *Aggression and Violent Behavior*, *34*. https://doi.org/10.1016/j.avb.2016.09.007

USAFacts. (2020). Who are the nation's 4 million teachers?—USAFacts. *USAFacts*. https://usafacts.org/articles/who-are-the-nations-4m-teachers/

## Chapter Two

Carmichael, S., Thelwell, M., Wideman, J. E., & Ture, K. (2003). *Ready for revolution: The life and struggles of Stokely Carmichael (Kwame Ture)*. Simon and Schuster.

Curry, T. J. (2015). *Facebook messenger*. Private Message.

Curry, T. J. (2017). *The man-not: Race, class, genre, and the dilemmas of black manhood*. Temple University Press.

Detroit Public TV. (2016, February 15). Kathleen cleaver interview | American black journal [Video]. *YouTube*. www.youtube.com/watch?v=sx0qIEi3QV8

Dillon, N. (2022, March 10). Rolling stone. *Rolling Stone*. www.rollingstone.com/music/music-news/chris-brown-rape-accuser-diddy-yacht-texts-1319017/

Estes, S. (2006). *I am a man!: Race, manhood, and the civil rights movement*. University of North Carolina Press.

Hudson-Weems, C. (2019). *Africana womanism: Reclaiming ourselves*. Routledge.

Luna, D. (2023). What percent of the population can bench 225? Less than you think. *Inspire US*. www.inspireusafoundation.org/what-percent-of-the-population-can-bench-225/#:~:text=As%20a%20safe%20bet%2C%20when,capable%20of%20performing%20a%20225

MacGill, M. (2022, December 23). *What size is the average penis?* www.medicalnewstoday.com/articles/271647#when-is-penis-size-too-small

Mutua, A. D. (n.d.). Multidimensionality is to masculinities what intersectionality is to feminism. *Scholarly Commons @ UNLV Boyd Law*. http://scholars.law.unlv.edu/nlj/vol13/iss2/4

Noël, R. A. (2014, November 5). Income and spending patterns among black households : Beyond the numbers: U.S. *Bureau of Labor Statistics*. www.bls.gov/opub/btn/volume-3/income-and-spending-patterns-among-black-households.htm

Tomassi, R. (2013b). *The rational male*.

Umoja, A. O. (2014). *We will shoot back: Armed resistance in the mississippi freedom movement*. NYU Press.

Walker, A. (1985). *The color purple*. Turtleback Books.

Whitaker, F. (1996). *Waiting to exhale. Fox home entertainment*.

## Chapter Three

(2017, July 3). Woman calls police on her baby's father . . . and claims that he 'beat' her in front of their kids . . . luckily he video'd the entire incident!! (wow . . . just wow). *Breaking News Live Media*. www.facebook.com/breakingnewsmedlive/videos/1968625666707668/

(2017, March 14). *Chimamanda Ngozi Adichie sparks debate about privilege with comments on trans women*. http://nytlive.nytimes.com/womenintheworld/2017/03/14/chimamanda-ngozi-adichie-sparks-debate-about-privilege-with-comments-on-trans-women/

Abrams, S. (2022). Black men's agenda. *Georgia Gubernatorial Candidate Website*. https://staceyabrams.com/policy/constituent-agendas/black-mens-agenda/

Araton, H. (2011, May 18). In book, Sugar Ray Leonard says coach sexually abused him. *The New York Times*. www.nytimes.com/2011/05/18/sports/in-book-sugar-ray-leonard-says-coach-sexually-abused-him.html

Associated Press & By Associated Press. (2017, July 12). Police mistake undersized woman for 5-10, 170-lb. Man, proceed to beat, punch her. *Atlanta Black Star*. http://atlantablackstar.com/2017/07/12/police-mistake-undersized-woman-for-5-10-170-lb-man-proceed-to-beat-punch-her/?utm_content=buffer144d1&utm_medium=social&utm_source=facebook.com&utm_campaign=buffer

Barnes, M. (2016, February 1). Judges say Black death row inmate is innocent, but he is still set to be executed. *Rolling Out*. http://rollingout.com/2016/02/01/judges-say-black-death-row-inmate-innocent-still-set-executed/

Brown, J. (2017, May 06) Graphic Photos Stir Doubts About Darren Rainey's 'Accidental' Prison Death. http://georgemallinckrodt.blogspot.com/.

Buchanon, P. (2015). *New money: Staying rich*. Hillcrest Publishing Group.

Carrega, C. (2017, June 29). *Brooklyn woman, hit man get life sentences in murder of her husband for insurance cash*. www.nydailynews.com/new-york/brooklyn/brooklyn-woman-hitman-life-sentences-husband-murder-article-1.3288761

Census of Fatal Occupational Injuries (Final Data). (2015). www.bls.gov/iif/oshwc/cfoi/cftb0295.xlsx

Curry, T. J. (2017). Lost in a kiss? The sexual victimization of the black male during Jim Crow, read through Eldridge Cleaver's the book of lives and soul on ice. In *The man-not: Race, class, genre, and the dilemmas of black manhood*. Temple University Press.

Curry, T. J. (2018). Killing boogeymen: Phallicism and the misandric mischaracterizations of black males in theory. *Res Philosophica*, *95*(2), 235–272. https://doi.org/10.11612/resphil.1612

Curry, T. J. (2020, March 3). *Facebook.*

Curry, T. J. (2021). Decolonizing the intersection: Black male studies as a critique of intersectionality's indebtedness to subculture of violence theory. In R. Beshara (Ed.), *Critical psychology praxis: Psychosocial non-alignment to modernity/coloniality* (pp. 132–154). Routledge. https://www.routledge.com/Critical-Psychology-Praxis-Psychosocial-Non-Alignment-to-ModernityColoniality/Beshara/p/book/9780367634636#

Dubin, J. (2016). *Trent Richardson says his family and friends spent $1.6 million in 10 months*. https://youtu.be/bGDUUMnFvwo

Ferner, M. (2017). *Officials ruled inmate's 'boiling' death an accident. But documents show they omitted key details*. www.huffingtonpost.com/entry/darren-rainey-inmate-death-dade-correctional-institution_us_58d94c9fe4b03692bea82e1b

Fletcher, W. A. (2014). Madison lecture: Our broken death penalty. *New York University Law Review, 89*(3). www.nyulawreview.org/sites/default/files/pdf/nyulawreview-89-3-fletcher_0.pdf.

Geiling, N. (2017). *No charges for Florida prison guards who allegedly locked mentally ill black man in scalding shower*. https://thinkprogress.org/darren-rainey-inmate-death-florida-93e39aadb651

Gender Harassment. *Title IX legal manual. Department of justice*. www.justice.gov/crt/about/cor/coord/ixlegal.php#D.%A0%20Sexual%20Harassment

Griffin, A. (2017, March 24). White U.S. army veteran killed random Black man with a sword after deciding to commit racist attack. *The Independent*. www.independent.co.uk/news/world/americas/us-army-veteran-james-harris-jackson-kill-black-man-new-york-timothy-caughman-sword-racist-attack-a7645736.html

Harriot, M. (2017, May 23). Black man found not guilty of crime, still sentenced to 7 years in prison. *The Root*. www.theroot.com/black-man-found-not-guilty-of-crime-still-sentenced-to-1795475956?utm_medium=sharefromsite&utm_source=The_Root_twitter

Hesse, J. (2017, July 14). Convicted of rape based on a dream, man relishes freedom after 28 years. *The Guardian*. www.theguardian.com/us-news/2015/dec/24/clarence-moses-el-free-denver-rape-case

Holley, P. (2017, February 11). A black man accused French police of raping him. Police claim it was an accident. *Washington Post*. www.washingtonpost.com/news/worldviews/wp/2017/02/11/a-black-man-accused-french-police-of-raping-him-police-claim-it-was-an-accident/?utm_term=.f8e207aaea69

hooks, b. (2004). *We real cool: Black men and masculinity*. Psychology Press.

hooks, b. (July 1, 1999). *Yearning: race, gender, and cultural politics*. South End Press.

Kaleem, J. (2017, June 17). A police officer kills an unarmed black man, and, in Las Vegas, there are no protests–Los Angeles Times. *Los Angeles Times*. www.latimes.com/nation/la-na-vegas-police-chokehold-20170519-story.html

Kristof, N. (2018, June 18). Opinion | On death row, but is he innocent? *The New York Times*. www.nytimes.com/2017/06/17/opinion/sunday/kevin-cooper-death-row-innocent.html?_r=0

Longman, J. (2016, August 19). Understanding the controversy over Caster Semenya. *The New York Times*. www.nytimes.com/2016/08/20/sports/caster-semenya-800-meters.html?_r=0

Mai, A., Marcius, C. R., Parascandola, R., Cerullo, M., & Mcshane, L. (2017). *Brooklyn day care worker beats her 4-year-old son to death with stick for dropping egg on floor.* www.nydailynews.com/new-york/brooklyn/mom-admits-fatally-beating-4-year-old-boy-brooklyn-home-article-1.2956011

Man Who Has Been in Prison For 63 Years, Rejects Parole. *Gives reason no one saw coming.* http://viralmadnews.com/man-who-has-been-in-prison-for-63-years-rejects-parole-gives-reason-no-one-saw-coming/

Miller, A. (2017, February 9). Michigan teen accused of sexually abusing her infant. *Mail Online.* www.dailymail.co.uk/news/article-4208444/Michigan-teen-accused-sexually-abusing-infant.html#ixzz4pMRk4kzL

Murdock, S. (2014, January 23). Darrin Manning, Pa. Teen, Allegedly has testicle ruptured by cop. *HuffPost.* www.huffingtonpost.com/2014/01/23/darrin-manning-testicle-rupture_n_4651700.html

Ng, A. (2015, December 17). *New trial for man jailed 28 years after 'dream' rape claim.* www.nydailynews.com/news/crime/new-trial-man-jailed-28-years-dream-rape-claim-article-1.2469667

Noble, M. (2017, October 3). UFC's Joe Rogan to transgender MMA fighter Fallon Fox: "You're a F***ing Man". *Bleacher Report.* http://bleacherreport.com/articles/1573044-ufc-joe-rogan-to-transgender-mma-fighter-fallon-fox-youre-a-man

Overpeck, M. D., Brenner, R. A., Trumble, A., Trifiletti, L. B., & Berendes, H. W. (1998). Risk factors for infant homicide in the United States. *The New England Journal of Medicine*, *339*(17), 1211–1216. https://doi.org/10.1056/nejm199810223391706

Phillips, K. (2016, August 31). An innocent black man was punched, Tasered and arrested by police officers. A jury awarded him $18. *Washington Post.* www.washingtonpost.com/news/post-nation/wp/2016/08/30/an-innocent-black-man-was-punched-tased-and-arrested-by-police-officers-a-jury-awarded-him-18/?utm_term=.f3f07c6efa58

Rothman, N., & Rothman, N. (2014). Why did kidnapping girls, but not burning boys alive, wake media up to Boko Haram? *Mediaite.* www.mediaite.com/online/why-did-kidnapping-girls-but-not-burning-boys-alive-wake-media-up-to-boko-haram/

Sacks, B., & Nashrulla, T. (2017, May 23). Here's what we know about Sean Urbanski, the alleged killer in the University of Maryland Stabbing. *BuzzFeed News.* www.buzzfeed.com/briannasacks/heres-what-we-know-about-sean-christopher-urbanski-the?utm_term=.xjeKagpwK#.gdPavqEBa

Safdar, A. (2017, March 21). Darren Rainey's death in prison shower 'accidental'. *Prison News | Al Jazeera.* www.aljazeera.com/news/2017/03/shower-death-prison-sparks-anger-170320181402828.html

Savali, K. W. (2017, May 25). Mistrial declared in trial of Texas cop who shot black man holding barbecue fork in his own yard. *The Root.* www.theroot.com/mistrial-declared-in-trial-of-fort-worth-police-officer-1795516414?utm_source=theroot_facebook&utm_medium=socialflow

Silva, D. (2017, March 27). White supremacist accused of killing black man hit with terrorism charge. *NBC News.* www.nbcnews.com/news/us-news/terrorism-charges-white-man-accused-hunting-down-black-men-n739146

Smith, W. L., Yosso, T. J., & Solorzano, D. G. (2007). Racial primes and black misandry on historically white campuses: Toward critical race accountability in educational administration. *Educational Administration Quarterly*, *43*(5), 559–585. https://doi.org/10.1177/0013161x07307793

Sommerfeldt, C. (2017, February 9). *Ohio woman allegedly videotaped herself raping 4-year-old boy*. www.nydailynews.com/news/national/ohio-woman-accused-videotaping-raping-4-year-old-boy-article-1.2968892

Staff. (2016, August 12). *New sports ad stars first transgender Olympian*. www.deccanchronicle.com/lifestyle/viral-and-trending/120816/video-new-sports-ad-stars-first-transgender-olympian.html

Staff, S. (2013, August 27). 6 stunning details we learned in Cowboys' Tyron Smith family saga. *Dallas News*. https://sportsday.dallasnews.com/dallas-cowboys/cowboysheadlines/2013/05/16/6-stunning-details-we-learned-in-cowboys-tyron-smith-family-saga

Steinmetz, K. (2016, May 2). Why LGBT advocates say bathroom "predators" argument is a red herring. *Time*. http://time.com/4314896/transgender-bathroom-bill-male-predators-argument/

Thompson, P., & MailOnline, B. P. T. F. (2011, June 30). A mother "killed her three month old son before taking his dead body shopping with her". *Mail Online*. www.dailymail.co.uk/news/article-2009571/A-mother-killed-month-old-son-taking-dead-body-shopping-her.html#ixzz4pMRSHQEV

Title IX Education Amendments of 1972. *Title 20 U.S.C. Sections 1681–1688*. www.dol.gov/oasam/regs/statutes/titleix.htm

Vâlsan, L. (2014, August 19). Boko Haram continues to kill and kidnap men and boys. The world is silent. *A Voice for Men*. www.avoiceformen.com/men/boko-haram-continues-to-kill-and-kidnap-men-and-boys-the-world-is-silent/

WeAllBeTV. (2015). *Judge Joe Brown: The Truth About Black Men & Child Support*. https://www.youtube.com/watch?v=Rn4BxAQVMp8

Wolfers, J., Leonhardt, D., & Quealy, K. (2015, April 20). *1.5 million missing black men*. www.nytimes.com/interactive/2015/04/20/upshot/missing-black-men.html?_r=0

Zilber, A. (2016, October 31). Murderer Joseph Ligon who has in prison since he was 16 REFUSES parole offer. *Mail Online*. www.dailymail.co.uk/news/article-3885440/He-s-long-Philadelphia-man-served-63-years-prison-crime-committed-age-16-refuses-offer-parole-instead-demanding-outright-release.html

## Chapter Four

(2006). African American suicide fact sheet. *American Association of Suicidology*. https://learn.devereux.org/srrp/Additional/AAS%20African%20Americans%20and%20Suicide,%202006.pdf

AAPF. (2023, April). #SayHerName. *The African American Policy Forum*. www.aapf.org/sayhername/

A National Epidemic: Fatal Anti-transgender Violence in the United States in 2019. (2019). *Human Rights Campaign Foundation*. https://www.hrc.org/resources/a-national-epidemic-fatal-anti-trans-violence-in-the-united-states-in-2019

All Cancers Combined, Death Rates by Race/Ethnicity and Sex, U.S., 1999–2011. www.cdc.gov/cancer/dcpc/data/race.htm

An Epidemic of Violence: Fatal Violence Against Transgender and Gender Non-Confirming People in the United States in 2020. (2020). *Human Rights Campaign*

*Foundation*. https://www.hrc.org/resources/an-epidemic-of-violence-fatal-violence-against-transgender-and-gender-non-conforming-people-in-the-u-s-in-2020

Beckett, L., & Clayton, A. (2022, June 30). 'An unspoken epidemic': Homicide rate increase for black women rivals that of black men. *The Guardian*. www.theguardian.com/world/2022/jun/25/homicide-violence-against-black-women-us

Benbow, C. M. (2022, February 7). Black male life expectancy hit hardest due to COVID. *The Grio*. https://thegrio.com/2022/02/07/2022-02-07-black-male-life-expectancy-hit-hardest-covid/

Black Life Expectancy. BlackDemographics.com. *Center for disease control and prevention, NCHS, National vital statistics system, public-use mortality files*. https://blackdemographics.com/black-male-life-expectancy-drops-6-years-since-2014/amp/

Blackstone, A. (2021, April 7). Black women are dying of COVID-19 at higher rates than men in other racial/ethnic groups. *Black Enterprise*. www.blackenterprise.com/black-women-are-dying-of-covid-19-at-higher-rates-than-men-in-other-racial-ethnic-groups/?utm_campaign=socialflow&fbclid=iwar0gxcxuaurvpiv1n4tjuikyq9saxesifvmmoro7pexelcdnybrxcm7s9iw&test=prebid

Brady, A. Chavez, N., & Pate, M. (2021). Gender differences in black youth suicide. *Research Brief, The Urban Education Collaborative*. https://thecollaborative.charlotte.edu/sites/thecollaborative.charlotte.edu/files/media/Research-briefs/2021%20Research%20Brief_Gender%20Differences%20in%20Black%20Youth%20Suicide%20.pdf?fbclid=IwAR0yOnHbTOyS64dxntONhTV-U8BRROZF5sbDLgbliF401GIPlc7UIEEKhoY

Cancer Mortality Continues to Drop in Females as Breast Cancer Reversal Looms. (2022). *MDedge ObGyn*. www.mdedge.com/obgyn/article/242851/gynecologic-cancer/cancer-mortality-continues-drop-females-breast-cancer

Carnell, Y. (2017, September 21). Straight black men are the white men of black people ???? Really?!?! 9/20 [Video]. *YouTube*. www.youtube.com/watch?v=8xc4K5UDDZs

Chason, R. (2017, September 30). 'Let the black women lead': Marches converge on D.C. to highlight racial injustice. *Washington Post*. www.washingtonpost.com/local/let-the-black-women-lead-marches-converge-on-dc-to-highlight-racial-injustice/2017/09/30/aa213ecc-a612–11e7-b14f-f41773cd5a14_story.html?utm_term=.34017f849559#comments

Child Maltreatment, 2020. (2020). *U.S. Department of Health & Human Services, Administration for Children and Families, Administration on Children, Youth and Families, Children's Bureau*. Child Maltreatment.

Fatal Force: 2018 Police Shootings Database. (2020, June 1). *Washington Post*. www.washingtonpost.com/graphics/2018/national/police-shootings-2018/?utm_term=.103e3ab2fa26

France. (2022, June 9). Black Americans bear the brunt of fentanyl "epidemic" in Washington. *France 24*. www.france24.com/en/live-news/20220609-black-americans-bear-the-brunt-of-fentanyl-epidemic-in-washington

Fuller, T. (2022, September 26). A rising tally of lonely deaths on the streets. *The New York Times*. www.nytimes.com/2022/04/18/us/homeless-deaths-los-angeles.html

Gramlich, J. (2022, January 21). Recent surge in U.S. drug overdose deaths has hit Black men the hardest. *Pew Research Center*. www.pewresearch.org/fact-tank/2022/01/19/recent-surge-in-u-s-drug-overdose-deaths-has-hit-black-men-the-hardest/

Homicide Rates by Race and Gender. (2020). *Centers for Disease Control and Prevention (CDC), National Center for Health Statistics*. [Chart] https://wonder.cdc.gov/ucd-icd10.html

Johnson, S. R. (2022, January 11). Study: Opioid deaths have surged among older black men. *U.S. News & World Report*. www.usnews.com/news/health-news/articles/2022-01-11/study-opioid-deaths-have-surged-among-older-black-men

Johnson, T. H. (2018, March 14). Silly rabbit, tricks are for kids: BLM was not for you after all. *Black Masculinism and New Black Masculinities*. https://newblackmasculinities.wordpress.com/2017/10/02/silly-rabbit-tricks-are-for-kids-blm-was-not-for-you-afterall-by-t-hasan-johnson-ph-d/#more-2694

Johnson, T.H. (2021, July 17). *The Erasure of Black Men: Flat Blackness, Flat Maleness, and the Olympics*. https://www.youtube.com/watch?v=3MOSgBLiGlM

Mason, M., Soliman, R., Kim, H. S., & Post, L. A. (2022). Disparities by sex and race and ethnicity in death rates due to opioid overdose among adults 55 years or older, 1999 to 2019. *JAMA Network Open*, *5*(1), e2142982. https://doi.org/10.1001/jamanetworkopen.2021.42982

Miller, E. (1988). The Rise of Matriarchy in the Caribbean. *Caribbean Quarterly*, *34* (3–4), 1–21. https://doi.org/10.1080/00086495.1988.11829430

Murphy, S. L., Xu, J., & Kochanek, K. D. (2013). Deaths: Final data for 2010. *National Vital Statistics Reports*, *61*(4). www.cdc.gov/nchs/data/nvsr/nvsr61/nvsr61_04.pdf

National Homeless Mortality Overview. (2020). *The national health care for the homeless council*. https://nhchc.org/wp-content/uploads/2020/12/Section-1-Toolkit.pdf

New HIV Infections Disproportionately Affect Black Gay and Bisexual Men and Black Heterosexual Women. (2019). *New HIV infections by race and transmission group*. U.S Department of Health and Human Services, Centers for Disease Control and Prevention.

Oluo, I. (2019). *So you want to talk about race*. Seal Press.

Patton, S. (2021, August 16). *Facebook*.

Patton, S. (2022, March 28). *Twitter*. https://twitter.com/DrStaceyPatton/status/1508481975430090760

Patton, S. (2023, March 4). I whup you, so the cops won't kill you! *Twitter*.

Ramchand, R., Gordon, J. A., & Pearson, J. L. (2021). Trends in suicide rates by race and ethnicity in the United States. *JAMA Network Open*, *4*(5), e2111563. https://doi.org/10.1001/jamanetworkopen.2021.11563

Reeves, R. V., Nzau, S., & Smith, E. (2022, March 9). The challenges facing black men – and the case for action. *Brookings*. www.brookings.edu/blog/up-front/2020/11/19/the-challenges-facing-black-men-and-the-case-for-action/

Sandoval, K. (2021, June 21). Suicide attempts are rising among young Black men. Experts say they face a "perfect storm" of hardships. *Insider*. www.insider.com/rise-young-black-men-attempting-suicide-perfect-storm-of-hardship-2021-6

Santhanam, L. (2021, February 18). COVID-19 has already cut U.S. life expectancy by a year. For Black Americans, it's worse. *PBS NewsHour*. www.pbs.org/newshour/health/covid-19-has-already-cut-u-s-life-expectancy-by-a-year-for-black-americans-its-worse

Schoenbaum, H., & Associated Press. Report says at least 32 transgender people were killed n the U.S. in 2022. (2022, November 16). *PBS News Hour*. www.pbs.org/newshour/nation/report-says-at-least-32-transgender-people-were-killed-in-the-u-s-in-2022

Staff, W. P. (2022, December 5). Police shootings database 2015–2023: Search by race, age, department. *Washington Post*. www.washingtonpost.com/graphics/investigations/police-shootings-database/

State of Homelessness: 2022 Edition–National Alliance to End Homelessness. (2022, September 27). *National Alliance to End Homelessness*. https://endhomelessness.org/homelessness-in-america/homelessness-statistics/state-of-homelessness/

Statista. (2023, February 1). *U.S. Mortality rates from cancer by ethnic group and gender 2016–2020*. www.statista.com/statistics/268602/cancer-mortality-rates-in-the-us-by-ethnic-group-and-gender/

Swaine, J., Laughland, O., Lartey, J., Davis, K., Harris, R., Popovich, N., Powell, K., & Team, G. U. I. (2022, October 18). The counted: People killed by police in the United States – Interactive. *The Guardian*. www.theguardian.com/us-news/ng-interactive/2015/jun/01/the-counted-police-killings-us-database

Tate, R., & Tate, R. (2023). Researchers sound the alarm over rising black male suicides. *DefenderNetwork.com*. https://defendernetwork.com/culture/health/no-way-out-black-male-suicides-rising-faster-than-any-other-racial-group/

Thornhill, T. (2019). We want black students, just not you: How white admissions counselors screen black prospective students. *Sociology of Race & Ethnicity*, *5*(4), 456–470. https://doi.org/10.1177/2332649218792579

Weeks, M. (2013). New UGA research helps explain why girls do better in school. *UGA Today*. https://news.uga.edu/why-girls-do-better-in-school-010212/

Xiao, Y., Cerel, J., & Mann, J. J. (2021). Temporal trends in suicidal ideation and attempts among U.S. adolescents by sex and race/ethnicity, 1991–2019. *JAMA Network Open*, *4*(6), e2113513. https://doi.org/10.1001/jamanetworkopen.2021.13513

Young, D. (2017, September 20). Straight black men are the white people of black people. *The Root*. www.theroot.com/straight-black-men-are-the-white-people-of-black-people-1814157214

## Chapter Five

10 Leading Causes of Death, United States. (2020). *National center for injury prevention and control, centers for disease control and prevention* (Originally work published 1999). National Vital Statistics System.

African American Suicide Fact Sheet Based on 2014 Data. (2016). www.wellspacehealth.org/wp-content/uploads/2016/10/African-American-Suicide-Fact-Sheet-2016.pdf

Average Sentence for White Male and Black Male Offenders Fiscal Years. (2016). U.S. Sentencing Commission, 1999–2014. *Datafile. USSCFY 99-USSCFY 16*. (Originally work published 1999)

Black Americans and HIV/AIDS: The Basics. (2022, July 22). *KFF*. www.kff.org/hivaids/fact-sheet/black-americans-and-hivaids-the-basics/#footnote-448622-3

Brady, A., Chavez, N., & Pate, M. (2021). *Gender differences in black youth suicide*(Research Brief). The University of North Carolina at Charlotte.

Browne, E. (2022, May 6). *'Stealthing' woman who poked holes in man's condoms sentenced*. www.msn.com/en-us/news/world/stealthing-woman-who-poked-holes-in-mans-condoms-sentenced/ar-AAWZmOZ

Center, D. P. I. (2022, October 1). Report: Black people 7.5 times more likely to be wrongfully convicted of murder than whites, risk even greater if victim was white. *Death Penalty Information Center*. https://deathpenaltyinfo.org/news/

report-black-people-7-5-times-more-likely-to-be-wrongfully-convicted-of-murder-than-whites-risk-even-greater-if-victim-was-white

Cherry, R. (2016, September 2). The jobless rate for young black men is a national disgrace. *RealClearPolicy*. www.realclearpolicy.com/blog/2016/09/02/the_jobless_rate_for_young_black_men_is_a_national_disgrace.html

Child Support and Incarceration. (2023, March 29). www.ncsl.org/research/human-services/child-support-and-incarceration.aspx

Curry, T. J. (2017). *The man-not: Race, class, genre, and the dilemmas of black manhood*. Temple University Press.

Dagan, D. (2018, March, 30). *Women Aren't Always Sentenced By The Book. And Maybe They Shouldn't Be*. https://fivethirtyeight.com/features/women-arent-always-sentenced-by-the-book-maybe-men-shouldnt-be-either/

Demographic Differences in Sentencing: An Update to the 2012 Booker Report. (2017, November). www.ussc.gov/sites/default/files/pdf/research-and-publications/research-publications/2017/20171114_Demographics.pdf

djvlad. (2022, November 24). Ed Lover on paying $6K per month in child support, Erica Mena complaining about $4K (Part 13) [Video]. *YouTube*. www.youtube.com/watch?v=_3bZAEJclOw

Douglas, P. N. *Black boys, black men, and suicide*. chrome-extension://efaidnbmnnnibpcajpcglclefindmkaj/https://health.maryland.gov/bha/suicideprevention/Documents/Session%201A%20-%20BLACK%20BOYS,%20BLACK%20MEN,%20AND%20SUICIDE.pdf

Joe, S. (2010). Suicide among African Americans. In *Oxford University Press eBooks* (pp. 243–262). https://doi.org/10.1093/acprof:oso/9780195314366.003.0014

Langhinrichsen-Rohling, J., Misra, T. A., Selwyn, C. N., & Rohling, M. L. (2012). Rates of bidirectional versus unidirectional intimate partner violence across samples, sexual orientations, and race/ethnicities: A comprehensive review. *Partner Abuse*, *3*(2), 199–230. https://doi.org/10.1891/1946-6560.3.2.199

Levs, J. (2015). *All in: How our work-first culture fails dads, families, and businesses–And how we can fix it together*. HarperOne.

McCormally, K. (2017). A 50-year plan for retirement savings. *Kiplinger.com*. www.kiplinger.com/article/retirement/t047-c000-s004-a-50-year-plan-for-retirement-savings.html

Prostate Cancer Additional Facts for African American Men and Their Families Guide. (2022). *Prostate Cancer Foundation*. https://res.cloudinary.com/pcf/image/upload/v1648050456/Additional_Facts_for_African_Americans_a866uj.pdf

Race and Wrongful Convictions in the United States. (2017). National registry of exonerations. *Newkirk Center for Science and Society*. www.law.umich.edu/special/exoneration/Documents/Race_and_Wrongful_Convictions.pdf

Robinson, J. (2019, February 27). The racist roots of denying incarcerated people their right to vote | ACLU. *American Civil Liberties Union*. www.aclu.org/news/voting-rights/racist-roots-denying-incarcerated-people-their-right-vote

Sandoval, K. (2021, June 21). Suicide attempts are rising among young Black men. Experts say they face a "perfect storm" of hardships. *Insider*. www.insider.com/rise-young-black-men-attempting-suicide-perfect-storm-of-hardship-2021-6

Slater, E. (2019). Actor and comedian Chris Tucker partners with the prostate cancer foundation during national minority health month to create awareness about the increased risks for African-American men and challenges them to "know the numbers". *Prostate Cancer Foundation*. www.pcf.org/news/chris-tucker-partners-with-pcf/

Spurling, D. (2021, November 10). How to destroy the black matriarchy featuring the Green Gorilla [Video]. *YouTube*. www.youtube.com/watch?v=U-mvqdExo50

United Nations. (n.d.). *United Nations office on genocide prevention and the responsibility to protect*. www.un.org/en/genocideprevention/genocide.shtml

Wikipedia Contributors. (2023a). Duluth model. *Wikipedia*. https://en.wikipedia.org/wiki/Duluth_model

Wikipedia Contributors. (2023b). Jury nullification. *Wikipedia*. https://en.wikipedia.org/wiki/Jury_nullification?wprov=sfti1

Winship, S., Reeves, R. V., & Guyot, K. (2022, March 9). The inheritance of black poverty: It's all about the men. *Brookings*. www.brookings.edu/research/the-inheritance-of-black-poverty-its-all-about-the-men/?fbclid=IwAR0PVhOpwDZ5IZvJplFlX_sq0cyXuNadoF1X09WycuqNX2poovbey4NENZ0

Women of All Races Get Shorter Sentences Than White Men. *FiveThirtyEight*. U.S. Sentencing Commission.

Xiao, Y., Cerel, J., & Mann, J. J. (2021b). Temporal trends in suicidal ideation and attempts among U.S. adolescents by sex and race/ethnicity, 1991–2019. *JAMA Network Open*, *4*(6), e2113513. https://doi.org/10.1001/jamanetworkopen.2021.13513.

# Index

Note: Numbers in **bold** indicate a table on the corresponding page.